PROPERTY LADDER
WITH
ALVIN HALL

ALSO BY ALVIN HALL

Money For Life
Winning With Shares
Your Money or Your Life
What Not to Spend
You and Your Money

CLIMB THE PROPERTY LADDER WITH ALVIN HALL

HODDER &
STOUGHTON

To Richard and Lucy
for the beautiful and welcoming
homes they create

Copyright © 2006 by Alvin Hall

First published in Great Britain in 2006 by Hodder & Stoughton
A division of Hodder Headline

The right of Alvin Hall to be identified as the Author
of the Work has been asserted by him in accordance
with the Copyright, Designs and Patents Act 1988.

A Hodder & Stoughton Book

2

All rights reserved. No part of this publication may be reproduced, stored in
a retrieval system, or transmitted, in any form or by any means without the
prior written permission of the publisher, nor be otherwise circulated in any
form of binding or cover other than that in which it is published and
without a similar condition being imposed on the subsequent purchaser.

A CIP catalogue record for this title is available from the British Library

ISBN 0 340 83366 1

Typeset in Berkeley Old Style by Hewer Text UK Ltd, Edinburgh
Printed and bound by Clays Ltd, St Ives plc;

Hodder Headline's policy is to use papers that are natural, renewable
and recyclable products and made from wood grown in sustainable
forests. The logging and manufacturing processes are expected to
conform to the environmental regulations of the country of origin.

Hodder & Stoughton Ltd
A division of Hodder Headline
338 Euston Road
London NW1 3BH

CONTENTS

1. Buying Your First Home: the Big Decisions   1
2. Finding Your Ideal Mortgage   23
3. The Homebuying Process   42
4. Home Improvements   59
5. Moving Up the Ladder   73
6. Property as an Investment   88
7. Managing Your Home Equity   102

   Index   119

ACKNOWLEDGEMENTS

Thanks to the following people for their diligent, thoughtful, and expert work on and contributions to this series of books: Laura Collins (for her brilliant copy editing), Emma Heyworth-Dunn (for her useful initial comments), Helen Coyle (who inherited this project and handled it and me with expert and caring skill, not unlike a midwife), Jonathan Drori (for giving me my first opportunity to do television), Daisy Goodwin (who hired me for *Your Money or Your Life* through which I gained many of the insights in this book), Stephanie Faber (for her expert publicity for my TV show and her ongoing encouragement and friendship), Richard Farmbrough (for being my always honest friend and for his sensitive production skills on the first three series of *Your Money or Your Life*), Emma Longhurst (for her great publicity work at Hodder), Vicki McIvor (for her dedication as my agent, protector, adviser, and friend), Robert McKenzie (for being true blue and generous with his knowledge and opinions), Gill Paul (for her initial efforts in helping to shape these books), Sarah Pennells (for her generosity, expertise, and wry sense of humor), Rowena Webb (for believing in my work and always being honest about it), Karl Weber (for being my trusted friend, my moderator, my spiritual inspiration), and, as always, everyone who appeared on *Your Money or Your Life*, *Investing for All with Alvin Hall*, *Save Me, Alvin* and other series I've done. Thanks for making me feel that my work was beneficial. Through these books I hope to share with others my knowledge of the practical strategies, insights, and benefits of handling your finances with focus, discipline, and a little fun. I know that each of you can make your money work in ways that will enable you to achieve some of the things we all desire – a debt-free life, a beautiful home, and the comfort of financial security.

Alvin Hall, London, April 2006

1 | BUYING YOUR FIRST HOME: THE BIG DECISIONS

Why Buy a Home?

The fact that you are reading this book shows that you are interested in owning your own home. Very likely you're among the thousands of people who are considering their first home purchase and are looking for a little solid advice. In these pages, you'll learn all you need to know about taking the first few steps on the property ladder, from the first home purchase to the upgraded home and, perhaps, the second home, investment property or retirement home.

The first question we need to tackle, however, is whether you're ready to begin climbing the property ladder at all. To start, let's consider *why* you want to buy a home. Here are three of the most common reasons people offer. Which of these comes closest to *your* main reason?

- 'Because a house is a great investment.'
- 'Because I want a secure base where my family and I can live.'
- 'Because paying rent is like pouring money down the drain.'

Let's look at these three reasons in order.

Is it true that a house is a great investment? It certainly *can* be. Between 1984 and 2004, average house prices in the UK rose by a cumulative 333%, while the FTSE All-share Index (representing the prices of most shares on the London Stock Exchange) rose by 330%. So during this 20-year period, a home represented a slightly better investment than the average company share – not bad at all.

But many people don't hold on to houses for 20 years. And during some shorter periods, house prices did *not* perform well as investments. For example, in 1989, the average house price was £70,400. By 1993, the same house fetched only £64,300. So someone who bought a home in 1989 and then chose (or was forced by circumstances) to sell it four years later probably *lost* money on the transaction.

The point is not that a house is a *bad* investment, but don't assume that a house is like a lottery ticket with a guaranteed pay-off. As with any investment, it takes thought, planning and research to ensure that your house purchase will be a money-maker rather than a money-loser. The advice in this book will help.

What about the second reason to buy, to create a secure base in which you and your family can live? This is a sound reason to buy a home, provided you think carefully about the meaning of the word 'secure'. Since 1986, some 640,000 homes in the UK have been repossessed because their owners couldn't afford to pay their taxes or mortgages. For these people, the security of homeownership vanished under a pile of unmanageable debts. There's no way you'll be able to enjoy the beauty, comfort, convenience and privacy of a home if you can't sleep at night for fear of debt collectors. So thinking prudently and intelligently about whether, when, how and what to buy is essential for anyone considering a climb on the property ladder.

This brings us to the third reason for buying – the belief that rent is wasted money. This idea is so much a part of today's urban folklore that I think it deserves a section of its own.

When Renting Makes Sense

I can understand why some people think that paying rent is a waste of money. After all, money you spend on rent doesn't accumulate for your benefit like equity in a home you own. On the other hand, the same is true of most other money you spend, whether it goes on water rates, council tax, electricity bills or a summer holiday. For some people, who aren't ready to become homeowners either financially or in terms of their life status, rent is a necessary and appropriate cost of living, not a waste of money at all.

Let me use my own circumstances as an illustration of the advantages some people may enjoy from renting rather than buying. When I moved to New York in 1982, I found a lovely apartment with reasonable rent, and waited many years before getting on the property ladder. Some of my friends were aghast, but while they scrimped and saved to pay their mortgages and maintain their apartments, I travelled all over the world to places I wanted to see. I was able to take chances with my career and grab opportunities when they came along – like the fortuitous meeting in London's Photographers' Gallery in 1991 that led to me presenting my first BBC TV series, *Alvin Hall's Guide to Successful Investing.*

During my almost thirteen years in rented accommodation, whenever the shower began to leak, or the window panes were rattling, or the heating went on the blink, I just called my landlord. I didn't have to pay buildings insurance or water rates or local homeowner's taxes. As a result, I had spare cash to start building my investment portfolio, accumulating shares, bonds and funds that have made me far more money since the 1980s than any property could have done. What's more, my shares paid me regular dividends, and my bonds generated interest payments. When you own a property, it doesn't provide you with current income (unless you rent out a room). On the contrary, you need to keep your chequebook at the ready to cover unexpected expenses for repairs or maintenance.

I finally bought a Manhattan apartment in 1994. At that stage, my rent had grown to be practically equal to the cost of a mortgage and the other expenses of owning. I had also watched a couple of cycles in the property market and established a stable financial set-up, which meant I wouldn't have to lie awake at night wondering how I would keep up with my mortgage payments.

What's the moral? Simply this: don't buy too soon.

Beware the Pressure to Buy

Several of the couples I've advised on my TV programmes got into serious debt because they bought property before they could afford it, or spent more than they should have. In part, I blame the pressure many people feel from family and friends to jump onto the property ladder before they're ready.

Property ownership seems to be regarded as a badge of success in the UK. The desirability of your home is intimately tied up with your own perception of your place on the economic sliding scale. A Brit who owns a home in a smart location always manages to slip it into the conversation at some point: 'Yes, I'm very handy for the Hampstead shops' or 'I've always been a Morningside person.' And many Brits I've known seem to consider it mortifying if they don't own a home by the time they're 25.

Americans aren't immune to house snobbery – even teenagers learn the subtle social gradations among various suburban communities around New York City or Los Angeles – but in my experience, they are not quite so hung up on owning property as the British. Perhaps it's because the United States is still largely a land of wide, open spaces, or perhaps it's because Americans are more likely to move around for their work, from state to state and even coast to coast. Whatever the reasons, most Americans are happy to wait until they are older and reasonably settled before taking on a mortgage.

The decision to buy your first property should never be an automatic one, and it should certainly not be a reaction to pressure from family, friends or society. It should involve many different factors, including where you are in your life, the status of your career and family, your overall financial objectives and the state of the property market. Helping you navigate this complex passage is the first and perhaps most important goal of this book.

Are You Really Ready to Buy?

To begin, answer each of the following questions honestly. If you're thinking of buying a home with a spouse, partner or friend, discuss the answers together. These questions will help you decide whether now is the right time to start on a property adventure.

Do you know where you want to live today and in five years' time? It may seem obvious, but buying a home makes sense only if you are reasonably certain about where you want to live for the next few years. The average time spent in a first property is seven years; if it's likely that you will need or want to move in four years or less, renting is probably the wiser option. Although property values generally rise in the long term, in the short term they may rise or fall unpredictably; therefore you run the risk of losing money if you need to sell a property quickly. (Perhaps you're thinking that, if you need to move, you can always hold on to the home and rent it out. Maybe so, but there are real pitfalls to entering the rental business, as we'll discuss in Chapter 6.)

Is your income secure? Many people leap to buy as soon as they achieve their first significant salary. This is a mistake. In today's volatile economic climate, jobs are less secure than you might assume.

Take a realistic look at your industry. If you lost your job tomorrow, how quickly could you find a new one? Do you have enough money in a savings account to tide you over in the interim? (I recommend keeping at least three to six months' take-home salary in a savings account for just such an emergency; the self-employed should also have an insurance policy that provides income protection in case of disability.) Contrary to what some people believe, the government will not pick up your mortgage payments if you are unemployed or too sick to work, for the first nine months. So plan now: how would you survive? If you don't have a good answer to this question, you probably shouldn't be considering a home purchase.

Are you debt-free? Don't think about buying a property until you have cleared all your other debts, including credit and store cards, student loans, bank loans and overdrafts. Mortgage providers will ask about your debts when you apply and may turn you down if your monthly repayment burden is too great. And even if a mortgage lender *does* agree to finance your home, burying yourself under a pile of debt that you can't comfortably repay is not a route to happiness. So, please, hold off from buying a home until your other debts are repaid. And if you need help with reaching that point, consult my book *Get Out of Debt with Alvin Hall*.

Is your credit rating strong? If you're not certain as to whether or not you have a good credit rating, check it. Write to one of the three credit reference agencies, Experian, Equifax, and Callcredit and they'll send you a copy of your credit report for a nominal fee. (You can find their contact details on their websites, www.experian.co.uk, www.equifax.co.uk and www.callcredit.plc.uk.) Study the report carefully. If you spot any errors (such as an ex-partner's debts being attributed to you, or even the debts of a previous tenant at your current address), send a correction to the agencies, enclosing proof if applicable.

If the report is accurate and shows that you have a poor credit rating because you've defaulted on loan repayments in the past or had a county court judgement against you, your ability to take out a mortgage will probably be impaired. You may have to work with a mortgage provider that specialises in poor credit risks (see Chapter 2), and the interest rate you pay will be higher than average. You may decide to wait two years or so and work to compile a perfect credit history during that time. This will improve your rating and better your chances of a low-rate mortgage.

Is your retirement savings plan on track? If you're in your twenties, you may find it odd that I should recommend thinking about retirement before buying a home. After all, you plan to work for another 30 or 40 years, don't you? True enough, but your financial priorities should still follow this sequence:

1. Pay off your debts.
2. Build up a three- to six-month savings cushion for emergencies.
3. Begin a savings plan that will provide you with an income for retirement.
4. Then consider buying property or investing in shares and bonds.

Think of it this way: everyone wants to retire one day, and nearly everyone eventually finds themselves too old, infirm or just plain tired to work. Protecting yourself against living your final years in poverty is a basic necessity of life – far more so than trading in a rental flat for a house and garden. Furthermore, when it comes to saving for retirement, timing is crucial. The sooner you start a pension plan, the smaller the portion of your salary you'll need to put away every month. The smart plan is to start in your twenties – and to make it a higher priority than buying a home.

Are you prepared for the financial demands of family life? Many people want a home, in part, to make a cosy nest in which to raise their children. It's a natural instinct and a good one. But if this is part of your motivation for buying a home, be certain that you're considering the homebuying decision within a realistic framework of other plans for your family. For example, if you already have children, have you begun a savings plan to finance their education? When calculating the size of mortgage you can afford, it's important to consider private school fees and university tuition as part of your broader financial outlook.

If you're planning to start a family within the next few years, this will affect your decisions in a host of ways. Of course, it means that you may need a larger home to accommodate those growing youngsters. It also means that family earnings will be reduced during maternity leave and perhaps beyond, as returning to work often proves difficult in the early years of parenthood. Therefore, if a baby seems likely within the next five years, I recommend you take out a mortgage no larger than you can afford to pay on *one* salary.

Have you saved a deposit equal to at least 10–20% of the property purchase price? With the average house price now around £200,000, this means saving between £20,000 and £40,000 before you start shopping, and remember, I'm referring to savings above and beyond your six-month emergency fund and your retirement plan.

This probably sounds like a daunting task. For most people, it will require at least a couple of years of disciplined saving – skipping treats, cutting back on holidays, wearing last year's coat for another winter or two. But if you don't have a minimum of 10% to put down when you buy, you'll be forced into a more expensive mortgage deal and will probably have to pay extra for a high loan to value fee, otherwise known as a high lending charte or mortgage indemnity guarantee (see page 36).

Have you talked through the financial commitment with your partner? If you're planning to buy a home with a spouse, partner, a friend or even a relative, you probably feel quite close to him or her, but even the best relationships can be wrecked when financial difficulties arise. We all grow up with quite different attitudes to money, and when those differences surface in times of stress, feelings of mutual disappointment, hurt, anger and even betrayal may appear.

Before you start shopping for a home, talk through the financial challenges. Who will be responsible for the mortgage payments, the council tax, the repair bills, the decorating and landscaping costs, and other regular expenses? What will you do if one of you becomes ill or disabled, or loses a job? What if you split up? (It does happen.)

Before you buy a home together, consider writing a co-habitation agreement that treats buying property together as a business arrangement, which, indeed, it is. (See pages 54–5 for advice on how to create such an agreement.) If your relationship is as strong as you think, it will only be improved by the honest communication that writing the agreement requires.

Is now a good time for you to enter the property market? In part, the answer to this question hinges on whether it's a buyers' or a sellers' market in your area. Are there 'For Sale' signs lining every street? Do your friends and acquaintances with properties on the market report long waits to find a buyer and disappointingly low bids? In that case, it's a buyers' market, which means you may be able to negotiate a bargain. By contrast, if decent properties are few and far between, and would-be homebuyers are making bids over the asking price, it's a sellers' market, meaning you may have to pay more to get into the game.

However, recognising whether the current market favours buyers or sellers isn't enough. You also need to consider your own circumstances. How long do you plan to stay in the property? How comfortably would you be able to survive an economic downturn? What if property prices drop by 20% or more during the next three years – how badly will that affect your plans? How about a similar downturn in rental prices?

The bottom line is that you should get on the property ladder at a time that is right for you. It's a decision that's very personal – but one that the questions you've just answered will take you a long way toward answering.

Once you've analysed your current position and your motives for wanting to buy, if you're still convinced it's the right thing to do, then you're ready for the next stage – working out how much you can afford to spend and starting to look around for that ideal home.

How Much Home Can You Afford?

Deciding how much you can afford to spend on a home involves some heavy-duty planning. The process starts with the basic formula that most lenders use to calculate how much you can borrow:

- If you're single, you can usually get a mortgage equal to 3.5 to 3.75 times your annual salary. So, if you earn £40,000 per year, you could borrow from £130,000 to £140,000.
- A couple with two incomes can borrow either a) 3.25 to 3.5 times their larger income plus one times their smaller income or b) 2.75 times their joint income. The two formulas will yield slightly different results. For example, if she earns £60,000 and he earns £20,000, they could borrow £230,000 using the first formula but only £220,000 using the second.

You may be multiplying your salary by 3.5 in your head right now. Add on whatever amount you have saved for a deposit and – bingo! – that's the value of the property you could own. But not so fast. Before you dash into the local estate agent's ready to make offers on houses, consider this reality: just because a lender will give you a loan of a certain size doesn't mean you can *really* afford it.

If you doubt this truth, take a look at the current high levels of consumer debt and the increasing numbers of people going bankrupt every year. The average British adult has consumer debt of £4,500, much of it growing by an interest rate of 16–30% a year. And since many people make only the minimum payments on their credit cards every month, we're going to see out-of-control debt rising rapidly for the foreseeable future, until more UK citizens learn new and wiser ways of using credit.

So rather than assuming that the mortgage amount suggested by the lenders' formula is right for you, dig a little deeper first. Figure out what your monthly repayments would be on the loan amount you're considering. You can do this by asking a mortgage lender to supply you with an illustration, or by using one of the many online mortgage calculators that are available. Here's a sample calculation I did recently using the BBC website property section (www.bbc.co.uk/homes/property).

Suppose you think you may want to borrow £100,000 to be repaid over a term of 25 years. A look at the financial pages of your daily newspaper shows that typical discount interest rates tend to be about 4.25% or the standard variable rate of up to 6.4% and most fixed rate are around 4.5%. (Be careful: as we'll discuss in more detail later, not everyone is eligible for the best current interest rate.) When you enter £100,000, 25 years and 5%, say, into the BBC calculator, you learn that your monthly payment on a repayment mortgage (the kind most borrowers should apply for) would be £591.27.

Your reaction may be 'No problem! I'm paying £600 a month for rent right now.' However, you're forgetting about all the additional costs of homeownership, such as council tax, buildings insurance, water rates, decorating, repairs and general maintenance. These must be factored in before you decide what kind of home you can afford.

In addition, the costs of buying can be substantial, especially if you buy a big, expensive house. There's a full list of these costs on page 57, but here's a rough guide. If you're buying a property worth £100,000, allow at least £3,000 for purchase and moving-in costs. For a property of £300,000, allow at least £11,000. And for a property of £500,000, allow at least £22,000. Over £500,000 and your costs jump up substantially, as you cross a stamp-duty threshold (see page 57). You'll be writing some mighty big cheques out of your current account during the buying process!

When considering the size of loan you can afford, don't overlook the possibility that interest rates may rise, and with them the cost of your mortgage. In the early years of the twenty-first century, interest rates have been unusually low. Over the last few decades, the average mortgage rate has been between

8% and 9%, with peaks and troughs along the way. Many experts are predicting that today's low rates will creep back up to more normal levels over the next few years.

Before taking on mortgage debt, use an online calculator to figure out how much the loan will cost if interest rates increase by 2%, 4% or 6% over their current level. Make sure you could still afford the repayments under those circumstances. Does this sound unlikely? The Bank of England base rate (used as the benchmark for many home mortgages) topped 12% in the mid-1980s and was over 14% as recently as 1991. It could happen again. And a few clicks of my mouse tell me that if the interest rate went up to 12%, the monthly payment on the same £100,000 mortgage would grow from £591.27 to £1062.49. See what a difference the interest rate makes?

'Never Mind the Expense, We'll *Make* It Work!'

People who've fallen in love with the idea of homeownership – or perhaps with a particular house that they desperately long to buy – sometimes decide to throw caution to the wind. They vow that they'll *find* a way to afford the home they want, even when logic and prudence dictate otherwise.

Some people defend their choices by comparing themselves to friends or family members. Having heard the rule of thumb that mortgage payments should be no more than 30% of your take-home pay, they point to acquaintances who are managing payments that amount to 40% or even 50% of their income: 'If Tom and Susie can do it, so can we!'

Unfortunately, the comparison may not stand up to scrutiny. Tom and Susie may have resources you know nothing about, a nest egg from an inheritance, for example, or income from a second job that Tom doesn't talk about. And if you spend more than the average in certain areas – for example, if you make maintenance payments, have a medical condition that requires non-NHS treatments, or help to support a parent or other family member – you may find that the amount you should spend on a mortgage is actually *less* than 30%, not more.

I've met people who ran into trouble by convincing themselves that they could economise significantly and devote the savings to their home mortgage: 'I'll go out to dinner less after I own my own home, so my spending on entertainment won't be so high', 'I'll stop buying clothes/books/DVDs until my salary increases', 'I'll take on freelance work to make up the deficit.' These may be good ideas, but sticking to such resolutions is harder than making them. After a year or two, if your will to save breaks down, you may find yourself with gradually growing credit-card debt and perhaps with missed mortgage payments – a formula for long-term heartache.

If you have your heart set on buying a home and recognise that economising is necessary to make it possible, launch your cost-cutting programme *now*, before buying property. Keep it up for a full year to make certain it's realistic. Then you can take out a mortgage and buy your home with the comfort of knowing you really can afford the amount you've borrowed. What's more, the money you've saved during your year of economising will enlarge your deposit, reducing the amount you have to borrow and trimming your borrowing fees.

Here are a few ideas you may not have thought of that can help you jump-start your cost-cutting programme:

- Drop that gym membership and keep fit by running in the park instead.
- Check the website www.energywatch.org.uk to find the cheapest gas and electricity suppliers in your area.
- Research the most competitive tariffs on fixed-line and mobile-phone accounts.
- Get competitive quotes for insurance and choose the cheapest policy that offers the coverage you need.
- Get rid of your car (or your second car) and use public transport instead.
- Study your newspaper's money section to make sure you are getting the best deals on your bank accounts, savings accounts and credit cards.

Some people plan to meet the mortgage repayments by subletting a room in their home. If you're in this category, be sure your plan is achievable. Check out the average rents for rooms in the area where you are considering buying, and don't assume you will get any more than average, no matter how desirable your decor might be. In your calculations, figure that there will be two months in the year when you don't have a tenant. People come and go, and your budget won't be their top priority.

My goal here isn't to discourage you from buying a home, just to help you make your plans realistic rather than emotional. If you're buying with a partner, encourage one another to be sensible; try hard to avoid the common syndrome whereby a couple egg one another on to ever higher spending expectations. Remember that, in the long run, your romance will suffer rather than flourish if you overspend on your love nest.

Street-smart Advice for Property Shopping

Once you've decided on the amount you can *really* afford to spend, you're ready for the fun part – shopping for your new home. Here are some tips that will help you make the most of the homebuying adventure.

Even people who know nothing about property shopping have heard the famous mantra 'Location, location, location!' The area surrounding a home is the single greatest factor in determining its value, today and in the future. So start by listing the areas in which you'd love to live and visiting a couple of estate agents in each. Half a day's touring of potential home purchases will help you decide whether you can afford the area you would really like to live in.

If you find that your dream neighbourhood is out of reach, explore the surrounding areas. Try to decide which are up-and-coming rather than beyond hope. When visiting an unfamiliar area, explore it on foot so that you can see what the atmosphere is like and how well kept the properties are. Is the paintwork peeling, and are the gardens overrun? Are there skips outside and fancy cars in the drive? How far is it to the nearest train station, corner shop or chemist's? If you're a keen gardener, which side of the road has the south- or west-facing gardens? Is there off-street parking, and if not, would it be easy to find a space nearby?

The quality of schools in a neighbourhood is another important factor to consider, and not only if you have school-age children. As school quality has a major impact on how well house prices hold up over time, even childless people ought to ask about schools when deciding the value of a particular home.

Once you've chosen an area or areas, visit as many homes in your price range as you can. Avoid the temptation to look at properties that are on the market for more than your maximum, even if the estate agent is whispering that the seller might agree to a deal. You'll be wasting your time if they won't drop the price sufficiently, and what's worse, you'll run the risk of exceeding your budget in a moment of weakness. When you find yourself (or your buying partner) on the verge of busting your budget, take a deep breath and try to imitate the dispassionate Mr Spock from *Star Trek*, warning Captain Kirk against some hare-brained scheme: 'But, Commander, that would be highly illogical.'

One way to avoid falling in love with an unsuitable house or apartment is to focus your mind on the practical features your home should offer. Make up a list of 'must haves' and 'would-be-nice extras' and judge every property you visit accordingly. Here are some examples:

> *Must haves:* three bedrooms, two bathrooms, a large kitchen-diner, a good primary school nearby.
> *Would-be-nice extras:* en suite master bedroom, a large, sunny living room, off-street parking, garden or roof terrace.

Keep focused on your must-have list, and don't let a beautiful view or a great conservatory distract you. If the place doesn't have everything on your must-have list, don't buy it. The glossy home-makeover programmes make it look simple to renovate or expand a run-down property, but if you need to knock down walls, add rooms, treat damp and install new electrics to make a house habitable, I say, be careful! Don't consider it unless you've got masses of DIY experience, time to spend and plenty of surplus in your budget. (See Chapter 4 for more advice.) On the other hand, don't be put off by hideous decorative schemes. That lime-green flowered wallpaper and fuchsia carpet can be replaced easily enough.

Construction quality is a different matter. Examine walls carefully for any signs of discolouration that could indicate damp, or large cracks that may have been caused by subsidence. Check that windows fit well in their frames and that floorboards are even. It will soon become law in England and Wales for vendors to provide a home information pack that includes a basic survey and other legal information concerning the property, so study this carefully and see if any alarm bells ring. (There is more information about the home information pack on page 80.)

Once you've found a property you like, go back as many times as you need to before you feel comfortable making an offer. Take measurements if you have any large pieces of furniture you want to fit. Check out the spaces for kitchen equipment, such as the washing machine. Make sure you can imagine yourself living there. If local school conditions are an important factor for your family, call to check that you would be within the right catchment area for the best school and whether there are likely to be places available.

And then – deep breath – if you're still keen, it's time to make an offer.

Congratulations! You're on the threshold of being a property owner. There's just one big hurdle left – getting the right mortgage. We'll tackle that step in the next chapter.

2 | FINDING YOUR IDEAL MORTGAGE

Unravelling the Mysteries of Mortgage-Speak

They speak in foreign tongues, these mortgage people. Sometimes I think the lenders like to baffle you by coming up with new terms for mortgage products in the same way that cosmetics companies herald new face-cream additives. If you're confused about the difference between a 'standard variable' and a 'discount tracker', and you're a little nervous about being 'capped', this chapter will help.

It's important to sort out the confusing language that the mortgage lenders use, since the cost of your mortgage makes a big difference to the ultimate cost of your home. Suppose you borrow £80,000 for 25 years at a rate of 6.25%. By the end of the term, you will have repaid £160,188 – slightly more than double what you borrowed! The lender has charged you the same again for the privilege of borrowing from them. So choosing the most appropriate and affordable mortgage is a crucial financial decision.

Of course, the best way to save on a mortgage is not to use one. But few people can afford to pay the full cost of a property in cash, which leaves no option but to take out a loan. The key is to shop around to find the mortgage with the best combination of terms for your circumstances and objectives.

Interest-rate Choices

The interest rate on your mortgage has a huge impact on the size of your monthly repayments. Most mortgage loans have a *variable* interest rate (a special type of this rate is called a *tracker* rate), which rises and falls along with a benchmark rate (usually one set by the Bank of England known as the base rate). Even an increase of a single point can boost the total you'll pay on your loan by tens of thousands of pounds. So one of the main concerns of most borrowers is to limit the amount of interest-rate risk to which they're subject – that is, the potential loss they face as a result of an increase in interest rates.

Fixed, *capped* and *discount* rates can all help to reduce the interest-rate risk you face. Here's how they work.

- A *fixed* rate, unlike a variable rate, is set at a predetermined level for a particular period, usually one to five years (rarely longer). After that period, your interest rate generally converts into a variable rate, moving with the benchmark rate. The benefit of a fixed rate is that you know exactly how much your mortgage will cost every month and can budget accordingly. Of course, if interest rates fall below the level you're paying while you are committed to a fixed-rate deal, you will lose out.

- A *capped* rate varies, rising and falling with the benchmark rate, but it cannot rise above a specified maximum. Although the initial rate will probably be a bit less attractive than with a fixed-rate deal, you enjoy the advantage of knowing that your monthly payments can't rise beyond a particular level, but you will benefit from any decline in interest rates.
- A *discount* rate is a special deal whereby you are offered a set percentage less than the lender's standard variable rate for a set period. Not all lenders offer such discounts – ask about available discounts when you're mortgage shopping.

All three of these deals can offer good value, but there are drawbacks to watch out for. You will often have to pay an arrangement fee – typically £400 to £600 – to set up the deal in the first place. You may be committed to paying the lender's standard variable rate for a couple of years beyond the lifetime of the special deal. And most special deals, especially fixed rates, may carry early repayment penalties, usually set at between three and six months' interest, which must be paid if you decide to pay off your mortgage early. These penalties may make it quite expensive to change your mortgage via refinancing during the term of the offer. So before signing on to any special interest-rate deal, be sure you understand the commitments you are making and the costs involved if you change your mind a year or two down the road.

The best combination of features is generally found with a fixed-rate mortgage. That's why I advise most homebuyers to look for the longest-running fixed-rate mortgage available. The certainty of knowing what your monthly payments will be for up to five years (or even longer) makes it much easier to feel confident about planning your family finances.

What About an Interest-Only Mortgage?

There is another crucial decision to make when you take out a new mortgage: the choice between a *repayment* mortgage and an *interest-only* mortgage. Here's the difference:

- With a *repayment* mortgage, each monthly payment covers both the interest you owe on the money you've borrowed (the *capital*) and a portion of the capital itself. At the end of a predetermined period (known as the *term* of the mortgage), the loan will be entirely repaid. Typical terms range from 10 to 30 years.

- With an *interest-only* mortgage, you pay only the interest due on the money you borrowed. This means that your monthly payment is significantly lower than with a repayment mortgage. However, you must use some other method to pay off the capital at the end of the mortgage term. This is generally done by investing a separate sum every month in the hope that the invested funds – either an endowment or an ISA (Individaul Savings Accout) – will grow quickly enough to cover the capital.

Endowments are managed by life-insurance companies and include an insurance component, which guarantees to pay off your mortgage if you die before the end of the term. In most cases, the rate of growth of the endowment will depend on how well the stock market performs, since the endowment funds are generally invested at least partly in shares or in unit trusts that own selections of shares.

As you can see, the interest-only mortgage offers a borrower the immediate temptation of lower upfront payments. But there's a significant risk involved – the possibility that your endowment may not amount to enough to pay off your loan. If that happens, you'll either have to find the money elsewhere or remortgage your home, taking out a fresh loan and starting the repayment process all over again.

Interest-only mortgages were very popular in the late 1980s and early 1990s, when the stock market was booming. At that time, many people assumed that the market would continue to sky-rocket indefinitely, boosting endowment values with it. Of course, that didn't happen. As a result, an estimated 80% of the people who bought endowment mortgages during that period are now facing a shortfall at the end of their mortgage terms, which can be quite a painful dilemma. Endowments shortfalls are covered in more detail in chapter 7.

One type of interest-only mortgage is known as a *pension* mortgage. You pay only the interest on your mortgage capital; then, at the end of the mortgage term, you are supposed to pay off the principal using a lump sum from a separate pension plan, a savings and investment account that you are responsible for setting up and managing.

For most people, I strongly recommend a repayment mortgage rather than an interest-only mortgage. When you rely on an endowment or a pension fund to pay off your mortgage, you are, in effect, taking on the risk of investing in the stock market – and betting your home on the results. With a pension mortgage, you are also relying on having a large enough pension, not only to fund your retirement comfortably but to pay for your house as well. Most people struggle with the first! If you are unlucky enough to have your mortgage loan come due during a period when the stock market is underperforming (as it did from 2001 to 2003, for example), you will be scrambling to find a way to keep your home. If you're forced to remortgage, you'll find yourself saddled with more repayments for years to come rather than enjoying the freedom and peace of mind of having paid off your mortgage.

Mortgage Term Options

The term of your mortgage can also make a major difference to the cost of the loan. Whatever the interest rate, the shorter the term, the lower the total amount of interest you'll pay during the life of the loan. For example, suppose you are borrowing £100,000 at an interest rate of 5.75%. If the term of your loan is 25 years, you'll pay £55,924 more in interest than if the term had been just 10 years. Think how useful that extra money would have been in your pension plan!

Of course, there is a downside: when the term of the loan is shorter, the monthly payments are larger. For a young person with a fledgling career and a relatively small salary, it can be tempting to opt for a long term of 20, 25 or even 30 years, with smaller monthly payments. However, the best strategy is to borrow for the shortest term you can possibly afford, even if the higher monthly payments are a little painful at first. As your career blossoms and your income increases, the monthly payments will become more and more manageable. In the end, you'll be delighted to have your mortgage paid off at the age of 40 or 45 rather than having to carry the burden of debt till age 55, 60 or even older.

For the Bad-credit Risk – Working With a Broker

You probably consider yourself a very trustworthy person. But you may not look that way to mortgage lenders. They will have doubts about you if you have a less-than-stellar credit rating due to missed payments, excessive debt or a past bankruptcy. You may also be considered a risky borrower if you are self-employed and have an income that varies greatly from month to month; if your employment history is spotty (for example, 5 jobs in the past 2 years, or 18 months with no job at all); if you already own other properties on which mortgages are being paid; if you need to borrow 100% of the property's value; or if you're getting close to retirement age.

In general, I would advise pretty much anyone to consider working with a mortgage broker rather than applying directly to banks and building societies for a loan. A mortgage broker acts as a kind of middleman, helping would-be borrowers link up with appropriate lenders. Good brokers often know about special deals that the average person walking in off the street isn't aware of, and they can help you take an overview of all the various products available from different lenders.

Before choosing a broker (or any other kind of financial adviser), shop around. Interview two or three candidates and get a feeling for their style. Here are some of the questions you should ask when considering a mortgage broker:

- *Are you an independent adviser, are you tied to one specific lender, or do you only deal with a handfull of companies?* An independent adviser will come up with the widest range of choices, while a tied broker can only recommend a mortgage from one lenders range. Some brokers only deal with a restricted panel of around half a dozen different lenders.
- *How do you earn your money?* Some brokers charge you a fee for their services, while others are paid a commission by the lender whose product you choose. If you'll be paying a fee, find out exactly how much it will be and whether anything is payable if you reject a deal they find for you. If the broker is paid on commission, they must tell you how much they are paid by the lender. Be aware that he or she may be paid at a higher rate by some lenders than by others, which could bias the advice you receive.
- *How long have you worked as a mortgage broker?* The longer the better. You don't want to be the client on whom the new kid on the block learns his or her craft.
- *What are your particular areas of strength and weakness?* Like every professional, a mortgage broker will probably be better equipped to help certain kinds of client than others. Make sure that the broker you choose has worked effectively with cases like yours.
- *What qualifications do you have* All mortgage advisers have to have passed an exam, called CEMAP (unless they are working under supervision). If your broker is also a financial adviser,

he or she may have taken other exams as well. The broker will also have to be regulated by the FSA to carry out mortgage business.
- *Can I call you on the phone with questions and concerns?* Some brokers discourage this.

The FSA maintains a list of all registered mortgage brokers. Any broker should ask you about your overall financial status, your short-term and long-term goals, and your fall-back provisions for paying the mortgage if you get into trouble. Beware the broker who seems quick to offer a one-size-fits-all mortgage plan with little regard for your specific circumstances. He or she is probably more interested in selling a lot of deals quickly than in helping clients make the wisest decisions for their own benefit.

Special Mortgage Deals

As I mentioned at the start of this chapter, new kinds of mortgage deals are constantly being invented. We've already reviewed most of the major variations you need to know about, but as you shop you'll undoubtedly encounter others kinds of deals that you may be curious about. Here's a round-up of some of the main products on the mortgage market, along with the basic information you need on each one and my advice as to its usefulness.

Cashback Mortgage

How does it work? When you take out the loan, you receive an extra cash payment, which you can use towards the cost of buying the house (fees etc) or something such as furniture. You may find that cashback mortgages (do not have the most comprehensive interest rates. lenders hope that first time buyers will be attracted by the idea of cash up front .

Who is it meant for? Cashback mortgages are generally marketed to homebuyers who are strapped for cash and want to be able to buy some furniture and redecorate after they move in.

My advice? Be aware that you could end up paying for the free cash in a more expensive rate, several times over

Flexible Mortgage

How does it work? There are over eighty different mortgages labelled *flexible*, and the terms vary a lot. Some consolidate your savings, mortgage and current account into a single account. This means that your savings reduce your total debt and the amount of interest you will pay over the term of the loan. Other flexible lenders will give you a credit line based on the equity in your home, and still others will permit early repayment or a short-term *payment holiday* with no penalties.

Who is it meant for? A flexible mortgage can be a good deal for those who have variable earnings and want to repay more of the mortgage in their cash-rich years, while paying less or even taking a payment holiday in leaner times. A flexible mortgage that consolidates your savings account with your mortgage may suit anyone who keeps a sizeable savings cushion for emergencies (which, as you know, is a very good idea).

My advice? The flexible mortgage has many benefits, of which the best is probably the elimination of early repayment penalties. But you should *avoid* a flexible mortgage if you lack financial self-discipline. The flexibility it offers may tempt you into putting off repayment, or using your equity credit line for current expenses, which is a dangerous, debt-expanding practice.

Self-certification Mortgage

How does it work? Those who are self-employed or work on temporary contracts may qualify for a *self-certification* mortgage, which allows you to borrow a larger sum than your current income would normally permit. Income checks by the lender are less stringent than with an ordinary mortgage, although you may be asked to provide a letter from your accountant or other evidence of long-term income. Self-certification mortgages charge a higher interest rate than standard offers, and you will normally need a desposit of 15%, although you may get a better rate with 20% or more to put down.

Who is it meant for? The self-certification mortgage is intended for the self-employed who don't have three years' worth of accounts to show, or those whose earnings are highly variable.

My advice? The self-certification mortgage is risky, both for the borrower and the lender. (That's why a higher interest rate is charged.) Rather than use this technique to push the amount you borrow beyond its natural limit, why not wait until you have three years' accounts to show and get yourself a cheaper deal?

Impaired-credit or Adverse-credit Mortgage
How does it work? Offered by a specialist lender, the *impaired-credit* or *adverse-credit* mortgage charges an interest rate significantly higher than any standard mortgage deal, so as to protect the lender against the greater risk of lending money to a person with a bad credit rating.

Who is it meant for? The impaired-credit mortgage is for those who've got into financial trouble in the past: those who've had a county court judgement against them, have defaulted on previous loans, had a property repossessed, or even been declared bankrupt.

My advice? Sign on for an impaired-credit mortgage only if you have no other option. Try to find a deal with no early repayment penalty, so that you can switch to a mainstream lender if you become eligible after a few years of good behaviour.

100% Mortgage
How does it work? This kind of mortgage involves borrowing all of the price of your home – in other words, putting down no deposit. When you take out such a mortgage, you'll probably be

required to pay a high loan to value fee, or high lending charge (HLC), calculated as a percentage of the amount borrowed over 75% of the property's value. For example, a typical 100% mortgage of £100,000 might require an HLC of £1,500 or more. The mortgage interest rate will also be significantly higher than with a standard mortgage.

Who is it meant for? The 100% mortgage is intended for those with no deposit saved up.

My advice? Please avoid this kind of mortgage by waiting to buy until you've saved at least 10% of your home's purchase price. (Better still, wait until you've saved 20%.) The 100% mortgage has two major drawbacks: one is the higher cost of the loan, as described above; the other is the possibility that you may end up with *negative equity* on your home if property prices should happen to fall. That is, you may find yourself owing more money on your mortgage than your home is actually worth. This will force you to come up with extra money – perhaps thousands of pounds – to pay off the loan when you are ready to sell. (See pages 110–12 for more information.)

Mortgage Protection Insurance
How does it work? Actually, this is not a special mortgage deal. Rather, it is a feature that most mortgage lenders offer – an insurance policy that will cover your mortgage payments for 12 to 24 months if you are unable to work due to accident, illness or disability. Premiums on this insurance are cheaper if you opt

for payments to start after 30, 60 or 90 days, or if you take out a separate policy for unemployment cover.

Who is it meant for? Those who are worried about how they would survive if they lost their job, had an accident or became too sick to work.

My advice? If you're self-employed, mortgage protection insurance is a good idea. (Actually, you need more insurance than this, so as to cover other living expenses as well as mortgage payments.) It can be expensive though, so shop around for the best rates on mortgage protection insurance rather than just taking the policy your mortgage provider offers.

My Eight Favourite Mortgage-shopping Tips

Armed with the information provided above, you're ready to tackle the job of shopping for a mortgage without being baffled by the lenders' confusing terminology and complex calculations. Here are some additional tips that will help you make the process rewarding:

- *Let potential lenders know that you are doing comparison-shopping for the best mortgage deal.* Aware that they are competing for your business, some lenders may offer you additional discounts or special enticements, such as fee waivers or refunds.

- *Be clear on every expense associated with your mortgage.* Make sure you know the interest rate you will be charged and what the monthly repayments will be, as well as any other fees or charges associated with the loan.
- *Read and understand the fine print.* Check the length of the loan, the early repayment penalty (if any) and any commitments you must make when a special deal (such as an interest-rate discount) comes to an end.
- *Comparison-shop for insurance.* As I've mentioned, some lenders tack a life insurance policy onto the loan; others ask you to buy buildings insurance through them. Before signing anything, compare costs to see if you can buy similar policies more cheaply elsewhere.
- *Get the most from your broker.* If you work with a broker, make him earn his fee by bringing several options to the table rather than just one hot favourite.
- *Ask questions, including 'foolish' ones.* If there is anything in the mortgage paperwork that you don't understand, don't be shy about asking for clarification and insisting on a plain-English response. Remember, the only truly foolish question is the one you are too timid to ask.
- *Seek expert advice if you need it.* If you're still confused about a mortgage decision, or feel troubled about the sales tactics used by a lender or broker, check the FSA's website (www.fsa.gov.uk). They offer useful consumer guides and information on how to complain.

- *Don't fret about saving every last pound.* The day after they sign their mortgage deal, most homebuyers spot one that's marginally better in the weekend paper. This will drive you mad if you let it. Do your homework before making a deal and find the best mortgage you can – then let it go.

When Should You Remortgage?

I recommend that you check how your investments are doing at least once a quarter. How quickly is your pension plan growing? Are your stocks and shares, ISAs, unit trusts and funds increasing in value? How much do you have in your savings account?

If you're a homeowner, you should add another step to your quarterly check-up: turn to the money pages of the weekend papers to see what mortgage deals are on offer. If the interest rate you're currently paying is competitive, fine – keep it. But if you are paying significantly more than new borrowers, it could be time for a change. It's possible that refinancing your mortgage could save you hundreds of pounds every month.

Unfortunately, it's not always easy to calculate whether or not remortgaging will be to your advantage. You need to take into account not just the amount you would save in monthly payments but also the costs involved in making the switch. the FSA's website has a special section 'The World of Mortgages laid Bare', which included best-buy tables and calculations. Other websites including www.moneynet.co.uk and www.lcplc.co.uk, have *remortgage calculators*, which will compare your current mortgage with other deals and tell you whether you would benefit from switching. Here are some things to consider in making this decision:

- If you switch lenders, will an early repayment penalty be due to your old lender? If so, how much? Check the terms of your current deal, find out the size of your redemption penalty and write it down.
- Some lenders charge between £75 and £150 for services like handing over the deeds and the administration costs of discharge. Find out and write it on your list.
- The new lender will need a valuation of the property, and a lawyer will need to handle the transfer. You may have to pick up these expenses (from £400 to £700) yourself, although the new lender may cover them as a sweetener. Make a note of this.
- Some lenders charge application or arrangement fees (£150 to £450) for fixed, capped and discount-rate mortgages. Check this out.
- If you borrow more than 90% of the property's value, you could be charged a high lending charge (HLC). See page 36 for a reminder of how this is calculated.

Add up the costs you would incur by switching mortgages. Then use a remortgage calculator to see how much the new rate will save you. Then consider: how long will the new rate last? If it's only a two-year deal, will you save enough to make the cost of switching worthwhile?

If it does look as though remortgaging will benefit you, approach your current lender first. Show them the competitive deal you've been offered and give them a chance to equal or better it. Many lenders will come back with an attractive package. If not, it's time to switch.

Now that you've become a mortgage expert – or at least enough of one to find the best deal for you – you're ready to move on to the next steps in the property-buying process. There's still more jargon ahead; but don't worry, I'll help you through it.

3 | THE HOMEBUYING PROCESS

From an Offer to a Confirmed Deal

Once you've located the home you want and chosen the ideal mortgage, you're ready to make the purchase. By rights, this should be the fun part, like buying a new outfit or an MP3 player. But the fun won't start just yet. In fact, some say buying a home is the third most stressful life event, exceeded only by a death in the family and a divorce.

Don't fret. In this chapter, I'll ease you through the complex and sometimes nerve-racking details that are involved in becoming a homeowner.

The first step is to make an offer on the home you want by phoning the estate agent who represents the seller. He or she will pass it on to the client and call you back with a response. And so begins the negotiating dance. Naturally, you want to buy the home at the lowest possible price, while the seller wants to sell it at the highest possible price. How both sides handle the coming interactions will determine whether or not the sale goes through – and if so, how happy both parties will be.

Conventional wisdom says that a buyer should start by offering 10–15% less than the owner's asking price. This approach is generally correct. There's a chance you'll succeed in capturing the property with a lower offer, especially if it has been on the market for a while, and in any case, it doesn't hurt to test the waters with a lower bid. If you are a first-time buyer, you have a bit of an advantage because you will be able to move in without having to sell another home first. From the seller's point of view, this reduces the risk that you may withdraw your offer, making you more desirable as a buyer. Having a provisional mortgage offer in place also strengthens your hand. Let the estate agent know, because these advantages might help you to secure the property in a competitive situation.

Let's say the agent comes back to tell you that the seller won't accept your offer. He or she may even hint that there's another buyer sniffing around. (It's against the law for an agent to *invent* other buyers to artificially raise prices, but a bit of exaggeration is hard to legislate against.) The next decision is yours. You can make another offer somewhere between your first offer and the asking price. If you really want the property, you can offer the full asking price. Or you can walk away and resume your home search.

This last option is the hardest one for most buyers. But it's often the best. Remember, there are always other houses, and it's very likely that next week or next month you'll discover another house you'll like even better than this one. So don't be afraid to back away from the deal. If you do, it's possible the seller may come after you, which will put you in a *very* strong bargaining position.

Above all, avoid getting into a bidding war against another buyer. That's a sure way to overpay, which will only lead to long-term grief. Steel yourself to say goodbye instead.

If your offer is accepted verbally, put it in writing and send it via the estate agent. Ask for a written acceptance of the offer from the seller and the removal of the property from the market. These steps will trigger the process of arranging your mortgage, survey and conveyancing, which I'll explain shortly.

How to Not Get Gazumped

The quicker you can confirm the purchase agreement in writing, the better, because until then you are vulnerable to a despicable practice called *gazumping*. You are gazumped if your seller accepts a higher offer *after* they've accepted yours. Unfortunately, once it happens, there's not much you can do except to chalk it up to experience.

You can discourage gazumping by checking to make sure

that the property has been withdrawn from the market. Ask a friend to call any agent who has been offering the property (not just the agent you've been talking with) posing as a buyer in search of the same type of home. If the agent proposes 'your' house to a new buyer, contact the seller directly to say that the agent they appointed is jeopardising the sale.

Establishing a personal relationship with the seller can also help. Call or visit the seller, express your happiness and excitement about your new home and say you hope to sew up the deal quickly. This message will make the seller less likely to be tempted by another offer. (The personal connection may also come in handy if you find you have a question or problem after moving in.)

As I write, the government is planning a number of reforms to speed up the homebuying process and prevent gazumping. From June 2007, sellers will be required to make available a *home information pack*, sometimes known as the seller's pack, which will include such information as the terms of sale, evidence of title, copies of any governmental consents and approvals given for the property, warranties and guarantees (if it is a new home), replies to local searches and a home condition report and energy-efficiency assessment based on a professional survey. These reforms should be helpful to future homebuyers. There's more information about these packs in Chapter 5.

Everything we've said so far applies to the English system for buying and selling property. The Scottish system is a bit different. Property transactions are handled by solicitors. A potential buyer starts the process by asking their solicitor to contact the buyer's solicitor and 'note interest' in the property. The buyer must then have the property surveyed, arrange a mortgage and decide on an offer. He or she submits a sealed bid by a specified closing date, which the seller will consider in competition with any other offers received. Once a bid is accepted, gazumping is almost impossible.

Other Ways to Buy

As of today, about one-fifth of all properties for sale in the UK are listed on the Internet. Looking at homes via the web can be especially helpful if you are moving far away and can't readily travel to view properties. Some property websites allow you to bypass estate agents and purchase directly from the homeowner. There's no reason not to buy online, and you may even find a bargain this way; since the seller will be saving the agency fee, he or she may have more flexibility to negotiate on price.

You can also buy properties at auction, another potential source of bargains. However, there are a number of dangers with this route. The successful bidder must put down a 10% deposit on the day of the auction, which means either handling the legal work, the survey and the mortgage *before* knowing whether your bid will be successful or taking a huge gamble.

For this and other reasons, buying properties at auction is not for the novice. If you're curious, visit a few auctions to see how they work and scan the website of the Royal Institution of Chartered Surveyors (RICS) for more information (www.rics.org).

The Next Steps

Once you've had an offer accepted, the next few weeks will be spent chasing up all manner of professionals whose services you'll need, including solicitors, surveyors and mortgage lenders. This can be a frustrating time. These are busy folk, and tracking them down to get your questions answered and push your purchase forward can be time-consuming. Try not to let the process drive you mad. Be polite but firm with all concerned. Return calls promptly and ask them to do the same. Send back any paperwork by return of recorded post or, if you are nearby, drop it off yourself. Above all, take clear notes of people's names and numbers, and maintain an up-to-date file with all the relevant papers. Being well organised will pay huge dividends and save you time, energy and sanity.

Working With a Solicitor

Buying a home requires legal assistance, which means signing up with a solicitor or licensed conveyancer you like and trust. If friends or family members can recommend one, that's a good starting point. If not, check the Law Society directory, which lists legal firms in your area (Tel: 0870 606 6575 or www.lawsociety.org.uk) or the Council for Licensed Conveyancers (www.theclc.gov.uk).

You can expect legal costs to start at around £500 for a property worth under £100,000 and increase from there depending on the property's value and whether it's *leasehold* or *freehold*. (A leasehold property entails extra legal work, because the solicitor must check every detail of the lease – more on this later.) You may want to get quotes from two or three different solicitors, but don't jump at the cheapest deal. A low fee could simply mean they keep their costs down by taking on lots of cases. Before choosing a solicitor, have a chat on the phone with each one and see which you find most reassuring, knowledgeable, experienced and friendly.

The work your solicitor will do when you buy a home is known as *conveyancing*. It includes the following:

- A check of the Land Registry to make sure the seller actually owns the property and that there aren't any impediments to its sale, such as debts from previous bankruptcies or an ex-spouse who needs to give permission before it is sold.

- A check of the property, or title deeds to uncover any irregularities you need to be aware of, such as official footpaths that cross the garden.
- A check of the lease to make sure there are no overly restrictive clauses relating to the service charge or repairs.
- A local authority search to ensure that there aren't, for example, any plans to build a motorway across your back garden or open a nightclub in the building next door.
- Liaison with your mortgage lender and, in some cases, the drawing-up of a mortgage deed on behalf of the lender, which sets out the loan conditions.
- Liaison with the seller's solicitor about the terms of the contract of sale.
- Enquiries about the fixtures and fittings that will be passed on with the property, details of any planning permissions, listed-building and building-regulation consents for work that has been done on the property.
- Arranging money transfers when you exchange contracts and when you complete the deal.
- Arranging for you to be listed in the Land Registry as the new legal owner.

As you can see, your solicitor plays an enormous role in making sure the home purchase goes smoothly. It's important to communicate with him or her openly and frequently. Ask questions, make certain you always know what the next step or two should be, and if you're worried about the speed or thoroughness of the process or are confused about any aspect of it, speak up.

Freehold Versus Leasehold Properties

As I mentioned earlier, properties in the UK are either *freehold* or *leasehold*. The distinction can be complex, but here's a basic summary of how it works.

When you buy a freehold, you own the property outright. Subject to legal and planning restrictions, you can basically do what you like with it. Most UK properties are freehold.

By contrast, buying a leasehold is a bit like renting a property. The owner (or *leaseholder*) owns nothing more than the right to occupy the specified property for a given length of time. Ninety-nine years is a nice, safe period that is common on residential leases. If the lease has less than 30 years left to run after the mortgage term has ended, you may find it hard to get a mortgage. The kinds of alterations you can make to the property will vary according to the lease, and other conditions may be imposed by the landlord.

In addition to a one-time payment to purchase the lease, the leaseholder must pay *ground rent* as well as a *service charge* to cover work on common areas (such as gardens, hallways and roofs). The landlord may also be able to charge you extra for major jobs like structural repairs or repainting the exterior. Your solicitor can tell you which of the common areas are your responsibility and which are the landlord's.

In a number of large cities in England, many flats and some houses are leasehold. If flats in a leasehold block wish to buy out the freehold, they can, provided that at the building meets certain criteria and least half of the leaseholders vote to do so. THe procedure can be costly and time-consuming (if the landlord does not want to co-operate). Once you own the freehold collectively, you will have joint responsibility for maintaining and insuring the building. For information on this process, contact the Leasehold Advisory Service (Tel: 020 7374 5380 or www.lease-advice.org).

Getting Surveyed

The next crucial step in home purchasing is obtaining a survey of the property. The most basic type of survey is generally called a *mortgage valuation*, since it is usually arranged by the mortgage lender, who wants to be sure that if they ever take possession of the property (for example, if you stop making your mortgage payments), it will be worth at least as much as you owe them. A mortgage valuation usually involves a limited physical inspection of the property by a surveyor or valuer to determine its value. As the buyer, you'll be responsible for the cost of the mortgage valuation, which is usually around £200, although some lenders charge according to the value of your property, so it can be more than this.

Here is where a major glitch in the process may arise. It's not uncommon for the survey to set a value on the property that is *lower* than the price you've agreed to pay. If this happens, you should try to renegotiate a lower price with the seller. You will be on solid ground if the survey has uncovered a significant flaw, like rising damp or a damaged roof, that needs to be treated. If the seller refuses to drop the price, you could ask that any flaws be rectified before the sale goes through.

In the end, you'll only be able to borrow up to what the surveyor says the property is worth. If the gap between the valuation and selling price can't be closed, you may have to put down a larger deposit to make up the difference – or back out of the deal.

If you are buying an older property (say 30 years old or more), I strongly recommend that you commission a more detailed survey, often called a *building survey* (formerly referred to as a *structural survey*). This will give you a fuller idea of your new home's condition and of any significant repairs that may be needed to maintain its value and usefulness.

Astonishingly, only 20% of homebuyers in the UK commission such a survey, perhaps out of a desire to save a few pounds

– it usually runs upwards of £500. This can be a costly mistake. I have a friend who bought a 100-year-old property in London over two years ago. Her mortgage valuation failed to pick up the telltale signs that the house had damp, mould and a serious case of subsidence. She has to pay for all the remedial work herself and still hasn't been able to move in.

If your property is less than 30 years old and looks in reasonable condition, you can choose a somewhat less detailed type of survey known as a *homebuyer's survey and valuation* (HSV). The cost generally runs in the £300 to £400 range, depending on the size of the property.

To find a surveyor, you can get recommendations from friends, the estate agent or your mortgage lender, or contact the Royal Institution of Chartered Surveyors (Tel: 0870 333 1600 or www. rics.org). You may save money by using the same surveyor your mortgage lender chooses.

Keep home surveys in perspective. A full building survey may list dozens of minor flaws that might needlessly discourage you from going through with your purchase. Before making any decisions, call the surveyor and ask him to explain the severity of the problems and the likely cost of repairs. You may find that problems that sound overwhelming when described in black and white can actually be repaired with relative ease.

Buying With a Partner or a Friend

A number of special considerations arise when unmarried partners decide to buy a property together. To head off any possible future conflicts, I recommend having a legal *cohabitation agreement* drawn up with the help of a solicitor. It will cost you a couple of hundred pounds, but it could save you a small fortune in the long run.

If this seems unromantic, please reconsider. A cohabitation agreement will protect both partners. Remember that couples, married and unmarried, break up every day. And though you may be convinced it will never happen to you, harsh reality says that it may. You owe it to yourself and your future prosperity to face this fact honestly.

Here are some of the key issues to cover in your cohabitation agreement:

- How will you split the costs of homeownership, including mortgage payments, taxes, insurance and maintenance expenses?
- What will you do if one partner is unable to pay his or her share of the bills? (Note that if one partner defaults on half of the joint mortgage payment, the other partner is legally liable for the whole debt.)
- What happens to the property if your relationship comes to an end? It's wise for partners to specify a *deed of trust with power of sale*, which means that a sale of the property can't be

blocked by one party. You can also require that if one partner wants to sell, his or her share of the property must be offered to the other party first at fair market value; however, if the partner is unable or unwilling to buy, the sale will go ahead.
- What happens to the property if one partner dies? Both partners should have wills, even if you are young and in the best of health. Otherwise, the sudden passing of one partner (in an accident, for example) may end up forcing the other to leave their shared home.

When friends buy a property without talking through the responsibilities involved, disputes that can shatter relationships sometimes result. I know two friends who went into partnership to buy a block of six rental apartments. One Christmas Day, Partner A got a call from some tenants to say the building's boiler had blown up. (Partner B was out of town.) Thankfully, no one was hurt, but getting emergency repairs done on Christmas was extremely expensive. Since the partners did not have a joint bank account for such purposes, Partner A ended up spending a lot of money from his own account. Upon Partner B's return, Partner A asked to be reimbursed, not just for the cost of the new boiler but also for the time he spent tending to the problem on Christmas Day. A lawsuit between the two partners ensued, which was only settled when they agreed to sell the property – and end their friendship.

The Final Steps: – Exchange and Completion

Once the work of conveyancing has been completed and the lender has confirmed their mortgage offer following valuation, the buyer and seller can exchange contracts. Through his or her solicitor, the buyer also pays a customary 10% deposit on the purchase price at this point. The deposit is *not* refundable if the buyer should decide to cancel the deal.

If you're buying a house, it's your responsibility to arrange insurance for the property following the exchange. (If you are buying a flat, you won't have this problem, because buildings insurance is handled by the manager of the whole block.) Shop around for the best deal rather than immediately accepting the policy recommended by your mortgage lender. If you're eager to reduce your insurance premiums, consider a policy that requires you to pick up more of the *excess* (that is, the portion of a damage claim that is absorbed by the homeowner). Make sure that the policy you choose covers the cost of rebuilding the house if it is severely damaged or destroyed, and that temporary accommodation will be provided if necessary.

You should also consider buying contents insurance, which covers your furniture and other property in the event it's damaged or destroyed by accident or mishap. Once again, shop around and get different quotes, including one from your buildings insurer, who may offer a discount if you buy both policies from them.

When you exchange contracts, a date will be set for *completion* of the sale. Completion is usually scheduled for about one month after the exchange (or less if both parties are in a hurry to move). On completion, the rest of the home's purchase price is transferred to the seller (generally in the form of an electronic transfer from a mortgage lender). At the same time, a series of other costs must also be paid, as shown in the following table.

Common Costs to Expect When Buying a Home

	PROPERTY COST		
	£100,000	£300,000	£500,000
Stamp duty	£0	£9,000	£20,000
Solicitor's fee	£500+	£600+	£700+
Land Registry	£100	£300	£450
Homebuyer's survey	£400+	£500+	£600+
Local search		£50–£200	
Mortgage fee (if applicable)		£200–£400	
Removal costs	Depends on quantity of possessions and distance travelled		

Stamp duty is a rather expensive little tax levied when you buy property. It can come as a shock if you are not forewarned. The tax equals 1% of the purchase price for properties costing between £125,000 and £250,000, 3% from £250,000 to £500,000 and 4% over £500,000. (Properties up to £150,000 located in an area labelled 'disadvantaged' are free of stamp duty. Check the website www.hmrc.gov.uk or call 0845 603 0135 to find out if your area qualifies.)

Notice that stamp duty gives you an additional reason for negotiating the purchase price if it means the difference between a higher and a lower tax rate. For example, on a house priced at £499,999, the stamp duty is just under £15,000; but on a house costing £500,000, the stamp duty is £20,000 – a full £5,000 more.

Your cheques for all the fees and other disbursements must be in your solicitor's possession before completion can take place. The estate agent or your solicitor will notify you when completion has taken place. You are then entitled to pick up the keys to your new residence (usually from the agent) and move in.

Welcome home.

4 | HOME IMPROVEMENTS

Did I say, 'Welcome home'? Perhaps I spoke too soon. You now have a house or flat. But it's not really your *home* until you've made it your own with colour, furnishings, lights and pictures that capture and express your style, your taste and your personality.

For most people, decorating their surroundings is one of the special pleasures of homeownership. But it's also a potential trap. Going overboard on home improvements is one of the easiest ways to run up excessive debt, which could convert your home from a joy into a burden and could even run the risk of losing it altogether.

In this chapter, I'll offer some advice on the *right* ways to go about fixing up your castle. Follow these tips, and every time you glance around your refurbished digs you'll smile with satisfaction rather than groan with dismay.

Take It Slow

The first temptation the new homeowner needs to resist is rushing straight into the local DIY store in order to redecorate from top to bottom.

There are many reasons why an overzealous refurbishing programme is likely to be a mistake. To begin with, decorating decisions made in haste are often poor ones. It takes time to get to know the character of your home – what it looks like in all weathers, various combinations of sun and shade, and every season of the year. And it takes time to know how and when you will use each room, where the bookcases and television and piano ought to go and which arrangement of sofa and chairs will produce the most sparkling conversations when friends visit. If you rush to paint and carpet too quickly, you may find yourself wanting to do it all over six months later. Instead, take your time. Make your decorating decisions gradually, test colours, fabrics and wallpapers by putting up small swatches or samples, and only make massive changes once you *know* you like them.

Of course, there are times when a property has some decorative scheme you just can't live with for a second – orange carpets and purple walls, for instance. If so, go ahead and change it on day one. (Hopefully you included the cost in your homebuying budget.) As for other changes, move in first and then set some priorities. Proceed one room at a time, starting with the spaces you use most often and then gradually finishing with the less-used areas. Most people need a full year to make their homes their own. Don't fight the process or rush through it – enjoy it and celebrate each milestone (new cabinets in the loo, matching rugs and curtains in the bedroom) with a special dinner or a bottle of bubbly.

And don't assume you can't entertain guests in a home that hasn't been thoroughly redecorated. Most people *enjoy* visiting family and friends who are in the midst of a refurbishing project. They get to reminisce about their own DIY adventures, recommend their favourite stores and contractors, and vote on the best colour scheme for the den or the baby's bedroom.

Decorating gradually will also help you avoid rash, what-on-earth-was-I-thinking choices. This is particularly important if there's a chance you may be moving on to a new property in three or four years' time. If you get caught up in some current design fad and install pink carpets, leopard-skin wallpaper or light fixtures made from driftwood, you may depress the resale value of your home. Instead, take it slowly and be guided by second thoughts, which are usually better than impulsive decisions.

Of course, decorating gradually is also financially prudent. It's all too easy to run up debt in the euphoria of new home-ownership. The excuses are ready-made: 'It's a new home, we need new furniture to match', 'Why have our own place if we can't decorate to our liking?', 'We'll be living here for years, there's plenty of time to pay it all off.' But furniture and fixtures are expensive, and soon the credit-card bills are too big to pay in full. The interest charges start to mount. You try to juggle the growing debt, signing up for new 0% interest deals and transferring balances from one card to another. But before too long, you'll run out of creditors who are willing to take you on (word gets around!), or you'll slip up and forget to make a minimum payment on time, thus incurring a heap of additional interest.

Running up debt is no way to start life in your new property. And as you'll see in Chapter 7, you can even jeopardise the security of your home if your debts get out of control. It's another excellent reason to redecorate slowly – as you can afford it.

Adding Value by Redecorating

It's a common mistake to think that you can cover the cost of home improvements with the amount they add to the value of your home. Some changes will increase your home's resale price, but hardly any cover their own cost. So redecorate for your own enjoyment, not as an investment strategy.

However, it makes sense to consider the resale effects of specific home improvements when deciding how much money to spend on them. The most important rule is this: *don't invest in property beyond the neighbourhood value.* Suppose you own a two-up, two-down terraced house in a street of other such houses. The chances are good that all those houses have market values within 10–15% of one another, and no matter how much you spend beautifying your property, you won't increase its value beyond that range. So be realistic in your expectations, and don't imagine you can turn your £300,000 home into a million-pound mansion by installing gold-plated fixtures.

Here are some specific ideas about how redecorating can add value to your property, depending on the existing price and market conditions in your area:

- Most houses already have central heating, but if yours doesn't, it will be worth the investment, usually recouping 100% of the money spent.
- Average cashback on bathroom refurbishings: 60%. Current wisdom is that simple white or off-white bathroom suites are most desirable, so get rid of those avocado and aubergine 1970s styles.
- Replace old Formica kitchen units with wood-fronted cupboards and marble-style worktops. If your base units are in good shape, you may simply be able to change the cupboard doors, drawer fronts and kickboards. Expect to recoup about 80% of what you spend.
- Double-glazing is a popular home improvement that will reduce your heating bills and probably recoup some 60% of

the cost on resale. Bear in mind though that in some areas especially with older properties, UPVC windows can reduce value. Insulating walls and the roof will produce similar benefits.

- If it's possible to add an en suite bathroom to the master bedroom, this is always popular.
- Sanded floorboards are perennially popular, so consider this if your boards are in good enough condition. If they're not, choose wood-strip flooring or a natural-fibre carpet in a neutral shade.
- Adding off-street parking to an inner-city property definitely pays (*if* you have the space available).
- Be very careful with cellar and loft conversions. If they look cramped or have low ceilings, difficult access and little natural light, they are better used for storage than living. On average, loft conversions only recapture about 30% of the money invested.
- Don't rip out good period features that give a house its unique qualities. Original Victorian or Edwardian cornices and moulding or Art Deco tiling and fireplaces are all worth keeping. However, 1960s and 1970s stone cladding, Artex textured walls and woodchip wallpapers are not! Judgement and taste are key.

Of course, whatever work you choose to do, try to design it with broad general appeal if you really want to recoup your costs. For example, maximise the natural light in the property and don't make any layout changes that block light. If a room is dim, use mirrors to direct the light and create a sense of additional space. And think twice about installing bold- or large-patterned wallpapers or tiles, which will limit the decorating options of future homeowners.

Paying for Home Improvements

If you've just bought a home – particularly if it's your first home – you've probably drawn down your savings account and are feeling rather poor. Under the circumstances, the temptation is to borrow against your own equity to finance those home-improvement projects that seem so exciting – in effect, increasing the amount of your mortgage debt.

Before you exercise this option, however, consider the dangers you'll be running. First, there's the risk that interest rates will creep upwards, taking your monthly repayments to a level you can't afford. Second, there's the chance that the value of the property may fall below the amount you've borrowed. This will mean you have *negative equity*, forcing you to come up with additional money – perhaps tens of thousands of pounds – to pay off the mortgage when you ultimately sell the house.

For these reasons, I urge you to pay for your home improvements out of current income if at all possible. However, if you're convinced you have plenty of equity in the property and that you can afford a *modest* borrowing programme, do the following sums to check whether you can afford to increase your mortgage (get help from your lender if needed):

- What would your monthly repayments be if interest rates rise to 8%? Could you afford them?
- If property prices plummet by 20%, would you still have equity left?

If you can answer yes to both these questions, then you can consider remortgaging.

As with any borrowing, hunt around for the cheapest loan you can find. Compare the APRs (annual percentage rate) of several lenders and check the small print to make sure there won't be any penalties if you repay the loan early. You'll generally get a lower APR if you are prepared to secure the loan against your property – in other words, if you default on the loan repayments, the lender can claim part of the value of your house.

Whatever you do, don't extend the term of your mortgage. Instead, choose the highest monthly repayments you can possibly manage. In this way, the loan will be repaid in the shortest possible time and you'll pay the smallest amount of cumulative interest.

The Renovation Adventure

Before you embark on any major home-renovation project – adding or expanding rooms, installing a new kitchen or bath or refurbishing a system such as heating, plumbing or electricity – be sure you know what you're in for. Do your research, talk to friends who've been through a similar ordeal and prepare yourself financially, psychologically and emotionally. Be realistic about add-on costs – for example, the cost of eating out while a kitchen is being gutted or the price of a hotel room for a week while your floors are being sanded and refinished. And assume that the job will probably take longer and cost more than forecasted; it almost always does.

Many people are unaware of the need to notify the council when embarking on a major renovation. You can't just pick up a sledgehammer and start knocking down walls on a whim. Neither can you construct a garage in your front garden, convert your loft or add a conservatory at the back. Most such projects will require permission from the local authorities. A bit Big Brotherish? Maybe. But they are concerned with crucial issues like whether any new structure is liable to fall down and injure passersby, stop passing cars from seeing a crucial road sign or pollute an underground water supply.

Local Authority Building Control regulates materials and methods of construction to ensure that buildings are safe and healthy to occupy. The same department monitors construction to make sure it's energy-efficient. Local councils grant two kinds of permission for renovation projects, one based on planning regulations, the other on building regulations. The two are separate and different, so don't assume that one implies the other.

In most cases, especially where a major project is contemplated, detailed plans and specifications must be submitted several weeks before you want to begin work. Throughout the project, periodic inspections and approvals may be required. If you live in a listed building (as determined by the Department for Culture, Media and Sport with the help of English Heritage) or a conservation area (designated as being of architectural or historic interest by the local council), the rules are even more strict.

Check out all the necessary regulations before you start. If you don't, you could find yourself having to undo all the work and pay a fine into the bargain. You will make it very hard to sell your house if you go ahead and do the work without having the relevant permissions, because your buyer's solicitor will ask to see them.

Working With Building Professionals

The regulatory complications are one of the reasons why it's important to work with an experienced professional when planning any significant home renovation.

If you are doing work that involves knocking down and building walls, expanding your property or moving kitchens and bathrooms, you would be well advised to hire an architect. They will know about planning permission and any building regulations that may be required, they will be able to spot potential problems that could affect your home's mechanical systems, and they will oversee the work of other professionals. Architects generally charge a percentage of the total cost of the work, and one of their roles is to keep the project on budget.

If a job is less complicated but still requires more than one type of professional (for example, a kitchen renovation, which involves a plumber and an electrician as well as a carpenter), then any good builder will manage the work for you. Here are some tips for choosing and working with a builder:

- Get referrals from satisfied friends.
- Look for a builder who has signed up to the Trustmark Scheme, supported by the government (www.trustmark.org.uk), or contact the Federation of Master Builders (www.findabuilder.co.uk or Tel: 0800152522).
- Get written estimates from at least three builders.
- Ask for references and talk to the people whose names and numbers you're given. Were they happy with the quality of the work and the service they received?
- Have the builder put your agreement in writing. It should

specify the work to be done, the materials to be used, the handling of waste materials, the completion date of the project and other basic parameters.
- Ask to see the builder's public-liability insurance certificate. Also speak with your own insurance company about any cover you may need.

For large building jobs, you may have to pay part of the fee up front and make some payments at interim stages. The payment schedule should be spelled out in writing. It's customary to hold back 5–10% for six months after completion, in case you discover crumbling plaster or another problem at a later date.

One more tip: beware of a builder who offers a 'special deal' based on non-payment of VAT. He may be a fly-by-night operator with little experience and few resources. If the job isn't finished or is done shoddily, you may not be able to prove that you had a valid contract and therefore may have no recourse.

If all this talk about working with professionals sounds troublesome, you may be tempted to tackle the work yourself. If so, be realistic about your limitations. By all means wield a paintbrush and try a spot of tiling, but don't attempt plumbing, electrics or any major construction work unless you're thoroughly trained and experienced. It's possible to do a lot of damage, which will cost a fortune to repair.

Keeping Up Appearances

Beyond the fancy stippling and sponging, the tongue-and-groove boards, the picture rails and the landscaped gardens that the magazines highlight, the most important thing you can do for your home is simply to maintain it in good repair. This is the best way to protect the value of your investment. Among other important steps to take, you should:

- Repaint exterior woodwork every two to three years to stop blistering and cracking, allowing rainwater to penetrate and rot the wood underneath.
- Clean and renovate heating systems annually or as recommended by the manufacturer.
- Have your roof inspected regularly and replace tiles or shingles when needed to prevent leaks.
- Keep plumbing fittings sealed and replace broken tiles in kitchens and bathrooms so water can't leak into walls or floors.
- Keep your eyes open for unexplained damage like staining on walls (a possible indication of damp) or tiny holes in wood (a sign of woodworm).

Keep records of the work you do. Some people keep a log in which they note all home-maintenance work, making it easy to check when the next work is due. This will also inspire confidence in potential buyers when you put the house on the market, and could be incorporated as part of your home information pack. If you have cavity-wall insulation, damp-proofing or wood-protection treatments carried out, keep the certificates for inspection by potential buyers. It's also worth keeping certificates that show that central-heating systems or built-in gas fires have passed inspections.

Does this all sound like a lot of work? Yes, but it's well worth it. Remember, your home is probably the single biggest investment you'll ever make. It's only common sense to spend an hour or two per month keeping it in tip-top shape – and making it a snug, comforting shelter for you and your family.

5 | MOVING UP THE LADDER

Some people, I suppose, pick a house the way they pick a spouse – for life. But for many others, the first home is just the bottom rung on a property ladder they hope to climb for decades, progressing from a modest house or flat toward the mansion of their dreams. (Actually, some people seem to pick spouses this way, too, but that's another story.)

If you've been living in your first home for a few years, perhaps you're ready to take the next step on the property ladder. Maybe you've been promoted, or got a raise at work, or you're moving in with a partner, or found out that you or your partner is pregnant. For whatever reason, when you're ready to move up to a bigger and pricier home, your goal will be to maximise the value of the place you're selling as you look for the next place to buy. In this chapter, I'll guide you through the process.

Prepping Your Place to Sell

If you're considering selling your home, you'll want some objective advice about what the property is worth and how to increase its sale potential. Of course, an experienced estate agent will have the expertise to give you specific guidance in this area. But even *before* you consult an agent, I suggest you do your own analysis and look for ways to boost the perceived value of your home.

Here is where an extra pair of eyes can be valuable. Invite your most straight-talking friend round and, starting outside the property, ask them to imagine they are seeing it for the first time as a prospective buyer. What faults do they notice? What strengths can be enhanced? Is there anything you can rectify or improve for a modest cost? Here are some specific elements to consider when seeking to maximise your property's curb appeal:

- Are the front garden, pathway and fence or hedge neatly kept or scruffy? Tidy them up and put out a few flowers in beds or pots. Make sure dustbins are kept tidy and out of sight.
- Is the paintwork on the sills and front door fresh and attractive? Flaking, damaged paint will make buyers jump to the conclusion that the property has not been well maintained.

- Is the entrance hall warm and inviting, or cramped and chaotic? Get rid of personal clutter – hats, boots, umbrellas, bags and so on. Install a high-wattage light bulb to brighten the first impression.
- Do your rooms appear neat and comfortable, or cluttered and confusing? Arrange books neatly in bookcases rather than leaving them on tables or in piles on the floor. Reduce the number of knick-knacks and collectables on display and put away small tables or footstools that block passageways.
- Does your house smell? Ask your friend: – you may have become oblivious to familiar odours from cooking, pets or tobacco. Open the windows to air rooms and put fresh flowers on display; avoid harsh chemical air fresheners.
- Do the walls, ceilings and woodwork look fresh, or dingy? Wipe down surfaces and touch up any chips in the paintwork. If necessary, repaint using pale, neutral shades, which create a sense of space.
- Are your kitchen and bathroom spotless? If not, do some scrubbing. Touch up discoloured grouting between tiles and clean limescale staining from baths and basins (if necessary, repaint them with ceramic paint).
- Are there other little problems that have gone unattended? If so, fix them up. Mend dripping taps, sticking doors, cracked windowpanes and holes in the walls.

You may also want to do some modest redecorating in advance of putting your home on the market. Think about your ideal buyers: what sort of people would they be? How many children would they have? Which features would they find especially appealing?

Now organise your spaces to demonstrate to your ideal buyers how your home will suit their lifestyle. Where will a computer workstation fit best? In which rooms will the family congregate to eat, do homework or chat? If you use a bedroom as an office or storage space, transform it back into a bedroom so buyers won't have to speculate about whether it will work. If a family room has been converted into a sewing room or hobby corner, put away the work implements and set out a sofa, coffee table and television. Make it easy for visitors to imagine being at home in your space.

Do the same with a back garden or roof terrace. You don't need to spend a fortune on plants or landscaping, but make the garden look neat and easy to keep. If necessary, lay a few new rolls of turf, chop back any overgrown plants and clear up heaps of debris or rubble. Consider setting out a garden table and chairs to show buyers the outdoor space they can enjoy in the summer.

The Lowdown on Agents

Some people choose to market their homes themselves, but most use an estate agent. How should you choose which agency to go with, and what should you expect from them? And why are agents the butt of so many sleazy jokes – is there any truth in the slurs? Let's find out.

The average homeseller feels let down by his or her estate agents. The reason is simple: most people tend to overestimate the value of their homes and the speed with which they should sell. When they're disappointed, the natural tendency is to blame the agent. Instead, try to adopt a realistic attitude – and avoid being in a position where you *have* to sell your home instantaneously. The less pressure you're under, the more patient you can afford to be.

To choose the agent you want to represent you, start by looking at the 'For Sale' signs in your street. Chat to the sellers about their experiences with their agents – the good, the bad and the ugly. Check out the agents who have local offices and pick some names from adverts in the local papers and free sheets.

Now consider the likely buyers for your home. Would they be locals? In that case, you should probably choose a local agent. Or might they come from some distance away? If so, widen the net by choosing a national firm. The Internet is a good way of attracting buyers from all over the country. Have a look at the websites of any agency you are considering and see whether they do Internet sales.

If you're located near the border between two districts, think about which area you'd prefer to be grouped with. Would you prefer to be one of the cheaper properties on an upmarket agent's books? Or would you be more successful as one of the better properties offered by a downmarket agency? There are no right answers to these questions. Your preferences will depend on your area and the type of property you have.

Choose a shortlist of five agents to visit your home and estimate its value. Ask them how business is going and what sort of prices they have been achieving recently for places like yours. Make up your mind how much you trust each agent. Which one would you be most comfortable buying a used car from?

When you hear the agents' valuations, don't leap at the one who quotes the highest price, especially if it's *much* higher than the others. The agent may be trying to tempt you with pie in the sky. Supplement the agents' opinions with your own research. Visit other properties in your area and consider honestly how yours matches up. Read the Land Registry quarterly reports at www.landreg.gov.uk to see the prices that properties in your area have been fetching.

Agents earn commission based on your home's selling price, and they usually get paid only if you sell the house through them. Some, however, work on a 'sole selling-rights' basis, which means they are legally entitled to their fee even if you sell the house privately – read the contract carefully. Some may also charge you if you withdraw at the last minute from a deal with a buyer.

Most agents will ask for exclusive rights to sell your house for the first few weeks it's on the market. Under this *sole agency* arrangement, the fee will generally be 1 – 2% of the purchase price, payable on completion. If the property is with one or more other agents as well, the rate will probably be 0.5–1% higher. (Think yourselves lucky, though. In the States, most estate agents take 6% of the selling price as their fee!)

Before you finally opt for one agent above another, ask them where and how they will advertise your property and whether your property details will appear on their website. And ask whether they belong to either the National Association of Estate Agents (www.naea.co.uk) or the Royal Institution of Chartered Surveyors (www.rics.org). Most agents belong to one or the other. Members of the NAEA have to subscribe to the Ombudsman for Estate Agents Scheme (www.oea.co.uk) and the RICS has its own complaints and redress procedure. This is an independent service for resolving disputes between estate agents and sellers, and it could be useful to let your agent know you've heard of it!

Once you've signed with an agent, help him or her to make up the property details. Make sure all the selling points are listed with the most beneficial emphases and that the photo of your property is flattering and taken from the best angle. Include one or two quirky, unique details if you can: a fish pond in the garden, a whirlpool bath, antique kitchen tiles or a stained-glass window in the hall.

The Home Information Pack

The agent should also help you to compile a home information, or seller's, pack. This standardised information pack is not yet required by law, but it will be from 1 June 2007, and it's up to you and your agent to put it together. Here's what it should include:

- evidence of ownership – from the Land Registry or copies of the deeds
- home condition report, including energy efficiency
- replies to local authority searches, indicating any planning permission, road schemes, water and drainage
- planning or listed-building regulations relating to the property and permission for any building works that have been undertaken
- any warranties or guarantees relating to damp-proofing or wood-protection treatments
- a sale statement – describing the property being sold
- if a leasehold property, details of the lease, including service charge, ground rent, buildings insurance and any special regulations.

Compiling this information will have a price, probably in the region of £600 plus VAT however, it is likely that in master cases you will only pay the cost on completion. But the availability of the pack is likely to speed up the homeselling process. Working with your solicitor and surveyor – ideally the same professionals who helped you when you originally bought the home – your agent should be able to put the pack together fairly quickly.

Be Your Own Agent

Would you like to save that 1.5–2.5% (plus VAT) that you would otherwise pay to an estate agent? You can do it by selling your home yourself and bypassing an agent's services. Here's how the process works. (Note: selling your home yourself isn't an option in Scotland, where a solicitor must act as agent.)

Based on your own research and analysis, decide on an asking price for your property, then erect a 'For Sale' sign (no more than 0.5 square metres) and place an ad in the local papers or shop windows. To reach a wider market, put an ad in *Loot*.

Produce your own printed sheet of details about your home, including a nice photo. (Get a sample sheet from a local estate agent and copy the format.) Also have sets of your home information pack at the ready. When would-be buyers phone to make an appointment, ask for a contact address and phone number, then post them the details and phone to confirm they've arrived. (This step screens out some con artists and others who aren't serious about buying a home.)

Show the home by appointment and make sure a friend or

family member is present for safety's sake. And of course, don't leave valuables lying around when you have viewings.

Once you decide to accept an offer, write a memo in which you note the sale price, any fixtures and fittings included in the price, contact details for both parties and their solicitors, and the completion date you're aiming for. Have your solicitor vet the letter as well as handling the remaining steps of the sale process through completion.

It will take you a fair bit of time and effort to act as your own agent. You'll need to be available to show the property upon request, and the paperwork involved can be tricky and time-consuming (especially for someone who has never done it before). Perhaps most importantly, you'll lack the objective guidance that an agent can offer concerning what your home is really worth, how to screen buyers, how to negotiate a deal and how to adjust your price demands over time. But if you feel prepared to tackle the sale on your own, you may end up saving a couple of thousand pounds – not a sum to sniff at.

When a Deal Breaks Down

Recent statistics suggest that, in England and Wales, 28% of home sales fall through *after* an offer has been accepted. When it happens, it's terribly frustrating, but whose fault is it? The buyer's? The seller's? The agent's?

Most often, the answer is no one. The cause often lies with someone three or four links down the chain who can't get the mortgage they need or whose survey has raised a problem with the property they are buying. (After all, in many cases A's home purchase is contingent on B's ability to conclude his purchase of a house from C, who is waiting to confirm his purchase of a house from D . . . and so on.) Usually you'll never know how many links are in *your* chain, but agents say that some chains are up to 20 transactions long! Perhaps the wonder is that so *few* homebuying deals come fall through.

The new home information packs should help a little, and the government may take other steps to alleviate the problem. One plan involves setting service targets for homebuying professionals including solicitors, local authorities, surveyors and mortgage lenders, in an attempt to speed up the process.

Lenders are also considering introducing 'chain-breaking loans' at terms more advantageous than the current bridging loans, which are used to buy a new property before the sale of an old one has gone through. Bridging loans can spell big trouble if anything goes wrong with the sale. A friend of mine recently had to take out a bridging loan when she couldn't sell her house in Dulwich, South London, and I don't believe she slept well for several months. She eventually had to lower the price on the Dulwich house just to get out from under the horrific mountain of interest. It remains to be seen whether chain-breaking loans will be any less scary.

If you find yourself waiting for a chain of transactions to fall into place, there are a few things you can do. Keep in regular contact with your estate agent, your solicitor and, if possible, your buyer. Nudge the process along as insistently as you can. If your agent can get in touch with other agents further down the line, he or she may be able to find out how strong the links are and whether there are any weak spots.

Above all, be prepared to be flexible if it will keep the chain intact, perhaps moving in with friends or family to let your sale proceed. You can understand why agents sing 'Hallelujah' when first-time homebuyers walk through the office door – after all, they have no other sale to complete before they can make their purchase. And you can also see why an agent with a choice between a first-time buyer and someone attached to a chain is likely to turn to the encumbered buyer and say, 'You are the weakest link. Goodbye!'

Having Trouble Selling?

Few things are more discouraging than having a home on the market for weeks or months without a reasonable offer. But don't panic, and above all, don't take it personally. There are several possible reasons why buyers might not be jumping at the chance to buy your home.

First, it may be priced too high. If you're not getting at least three viewings a week, your asking price is probably too expensive. Ask your agent about the feedback he or she is getting. If more than two potential buyers have said it costs too much, then they're right – it does. Most potential buyers will not try to negotiate a lower price; they'll simply skip your home and move on to other properties.

Re-examine the basis for your price. Perhaps conditions in the neighbourhood have changed, or the features you thought would generate interest have proven to be unenticing. Reduce your asking price by 5–10% and see whether this makes a difference to the traffic generated.

What if buyers are visiting your home but not making offers? Ask your agent what's putting them off. You might want to show a few buyers round yourself and watch their reactions closely. Don't oversell but simply mention how you use each room, then stand back and give them the space to look. If there are any features you want to highlight, such as a great view from a window, make sure you pause so they can notice. Watch the glances that dart back and forth between couples, if you can. Is there an obvious sticking point? After a few such visits, you may be able to tell which rooms are causing problems – and perhaps fix matters with a fresh coat of paint, improved lighting or a better arrangement of the furniture.

What if you've had an offer that fell through after the survey? Most likely one or two serious faults were highlighted by the surveyor – a leaky roof, a wheezing furnace, sub-standard electrics. If this is the case, bite the bullet and do the necessary work. It may cost you a few thousand pounds, but it will probably save you money in the long run.

Finally, what if you suspect that your agent is at fault? Be sure you've given him or her a fair chance to sell the property – six weeks at a minimum – then bring in another agent and see if he or she can make a difference with new clientele and a fresh approach.

The Art of the Close

The best salespeople are masters at the 'close', the gentle art of nudging a potential buyer across the finish line. If you have a would-be homebuyer nibbling at your property but refusing to swallow the hook, there are a few things you can do to help close the deal:

- Ask your agent about the buyer's background and research the kind of local information they may appreciate. For example, look up train times to the city centre, confirm the catchment area for local schools or research how much they could collect by renting out a room.
- Consider what you love about living in the area and pass it on. Display a photo album of community events (the annual fair, the holiday concert), a collection of brochures from the

best local stores or maps of nearby parks and nature trails.
- Reassure a potential buyer that you abhor the practice of gazumping and won't consider any other offers that come in after you've accepted theirs.
- Offer to pay the buyer's survey costs, throw in those curtains she admired or knock a tiny bit (1–2%) off the price. Make the buyer feel that he or she is coming out of the deal as the winner.

And what if you are in the happy position of getting more than one offer on your home? Don't automatically choose the highest bid. First, ask your estate agent to explore which buyers are in a chain and who is in the best position to close the deal swiftly and cleanly. Don't be swayed by your sympathy for that nice couple with the three toddlers who were really desperate for your house but may not be able to exchange for months, otherwise you may find you've taken their troubles and made them your own.

And as soon as you accept an offer, you need to accelerate your efforts to buy your *next* place. Whatever you do, keep the chain intact! That's how the property-ladder game is played.

6| PROPERTY AS AN INVESTMENT

You're feeling rather confident about this property business. You bought a starter home, you enjoyed living in it for a few years, you fixed it up a bit and resold it for a little profit – enough to let you move into a nicer, pricier place. You've had a bit of a paddle, and all seems to be going well. Why not go for a proper swim?

Nowadays millions of people in the UK (and elsewhere) are thinking about property ownership as a great way to invest and make their money grow. It's not surprising. After all, in recent years – even as the shares market has been in the doldrums – property values have grown steadily, earning big returns for people who put their savings into property. So buying a second home as a holiday spot, as a rental unit or to refurbish and resell may seem like a tempting notion.

Property *can* be a good investment, but it has a serious downside as well. In today's era of property euphoria, it's important for me to spell out the drawbacks and risks associated with property investments.

First, remember that property is not a liquid investment – that is, you can't assume that a house or flat you own can be sold for its full market value at a moment's notice. (By contrast, shares, bonds and bank accounts *are* liquid, because you can sell them at market value at any time.) Therefore, you don't want to invest money in property that you might need in the next ten years – for example, the emergency fund you've set aside in case of an illness, accident or job loss.

Second, be aware that house prices don't *always* rise. Sometimes they remain flat or even fall for years at a time, particularly during times when interest rates are rising. (Rising rates make mortgages more expensive and discourage homebuying.) So don't assume that a property investment is some kind of magic beanstalk guaranteed to grow. The Financial Services Authority has recently been warning that people may be putting too much faith in property as an investment and they could get seriously burned the next time prices fall.

Third, consider some of the drawbacks of property compared with other investments. Unlike shares, bonds or bank accounts, property generates no interest, dividends or other regular income. Instead, you must invest money (as well as time and energy) in keeping up the property – all with no guarantee of a return on your investment.

Obviously, there are plenty of people who have made serious

money from property, but there are some big losers, too. The difference is that you don't hear the losers bragging about it at parties! In this chapter, I'll outline both the potential benefits and the pitfalls of buying property as an investment. If you still want to take the plunge after reading these pages, fine – so long as you go in with both eyes open.

Investing in a Home from Home

One of the most popular ways to get started in property investing is by buying a second home for holidays and, ultimately, retirement. Why not? Everyone who has treasured a week at the beach or in the country has fantasised about owning a thatched cottage or seaside apartment like the one they've enjoyed on holiday. And if a second home can also be a source of investment profit, who wouldn't be interested?

But owning a second home isn't right for everyone. Here are some of the questions you need to ask youself before following this route:

- *Will you use your second home often enough to oversee its maintenance and make the costs worthwhile?* Be realistic about this. Most people have jobs that keep them tied to their first homes nearly year-round. And even a relatively short three- or four-hour drive to a seaside cottage or a house in the country may become wearying when done regularly. I know couples who've bought their country cottage and now groan under the obligation of visiting it frequently enough to keep it from disintegrating with neglect. One man complained to me that his picturesque house by the seashore needs to be repainted every single year to protect it from the salt air. It's a lot of money and work to invest for just a fortnight's pleasure.

- *How will you finance your second home?* Raising the money to buy your second home will be the first hurdle. If you have a huge amount of equity in your first home, you can talk to your mortgage lender about adding the new property onto your loan. But as you know, increasing the amount you owe is always fraught with risk. One problem is that properties (including second homes) have a way of generating unexpected costs. I know a London couple who took out 80% of the equity in their city flat to buy a country house. Once they took possession, however, they found it needed a lot of work – work they couldn't pay for because of the size of the loan they were repaying. They ended up struggling to do the work themselves, investing their weekends in carpentry, roofing and painting rather than leisure.

- Even a house that's in good shape creates financial demands. For example, you'll need to buy a brand-new set of furniture and household goods – everything from sheets and towels to cutlery and coffee mugs. These things add up, usually into thousands of pounds.

- My advice: be careful about expanding your debt to pay for a second home. Keep an equity cushion of at least 40% of your first property's value.
- *Have you drawn up a realistic budget?* Before deciding to buy a second home, make up a revised monthly budget that reflects all the new costs you'll be carrying. Include not only your mortgage payments but also the double sets of utility bills, insurance premiums, repairs and general upkeep of the second property. Since 2004, council tax will also take a bigger bite. Instead of getting a 50% tax reduction on a second property (as under previous law), you may now get only 10%.
- *Have you thoroughly researched your second property?* Just as when you buy your primary residence, you want to be sure that your second home is fairly priced and located in an area where property values are likely to rise in the future. This takes careful planning and research, something that may be hard to do from a distance. Before buying a home in a resort community or rural paradise, try to spend more than a week or two in the area. Settle in for a month or more, immerse yourself in the realities of local life – shopping, doctor visits, car repairs – and study the property market. Don't buy until you're convinced of the long-term economic strength of the community.

If you follow these principles, you'll stand a much better chance of really enjoying your home from home – and earning a profit on the property when it comes time to sell.

Buying Property Overseas

Another fantasy shared by many Britons is the idea of buying a second home in some sunny clime – Portugal, Greece, Italy or the Caribbean, for example. Again, it's an idea that *may* work well, provided you do your research.

As I've explained in this book, buying property is a complex financial and legal matter with plenty of room for things to go wrong, even here in the UK. When you buy in a foreign land, the potential complications are multiplied. The seller and his agent may not speak English, or may develop a case of selective incomprehension at moments of maximum inconvenience to you! Laws, regulations and customs vary, and finding someone reliable to explain local practices may be difficult or impossible. And simply being hundreds or thousands of miles away from the action inevitably makes any transaction more difficult and prone to confusion.

For these reasons, I'm always flabbergasted when I hear of people who can't even order a grilled cheese sandwich and a coffee in another language trying to buy a property overseas. It's a risky venture not to be entered into lightly.

Here are some of the complications you may face when you try to buy a foreign property:

- **It's easy to be blind-sided by local laws.** For example, before buying a home in Spain, you will be caught by Spanish inheritance laws unless you make out a will – in Spain.

- In some countries, a new homeowner may be legally responsible for debts left behind by the previous owner.
- To protect your rights, you' should appoint your own lawyer and in some countries you will need: a fiscal representative as well.
- Many sellers of Spanish properties mysteriously don't seem to hold the title deeds or *escritura*. Steer clear! Buy a place without its papers and you'll be entering a legal hinterland in which you could be stuck for years to come.
- Don't assume that foreign property is a good way of avoiding UK taxes. For example many Britons were advised to buy properties in Portugal using holding companies to avoid tax, but the Portuegse government impose an extra charge on those who did – designed to wipe out the tax savings.

Local estate agents who sell properties to British clients are often fluent in English as well as knowledgeable about local practices. But remember that, like all estate agents, they represent the interests of the seller, not the buyer, so the rosy scenarios they may paint for you need to be taken with a pinch of salt. For example, an agent may tell you that the home you're considering will easily pay for itself through rental income. This is possible, but unlikely. A nice seaside property may attract tenants for a couple of weeks over Easter and then again in July and August – maybe 11 or 12 weeks in total. And if you want to spend any time there yourself during those months, you'll be reducing your possible income. Furthermore, there's very high wear-and-tear in holiday rental property. If you don't repaint and overhaul every year, the place will deteriorate fast. All in all, it's dangerous to assume that rental income will make much of a dent in your expenses.

Finally, never buy an overseas property on the spur of the moment, while you're riding the wave of holiday *joie de vivre* and still under the influence of that lunchtime jug of sangria. Come home and let the tan fade a while. Sort out your finances and figure out whether you can really afford an overseas money pit (even one with a glorious view and great weather). And as I recommended on page 92 when discussing second homes, it's important to spend a good bit of time in the area where you are planning to buy before making any decision. It's one thing to cope with language difficulties, cultural differences, strange foods and customs, and the sheer practical challenges of living abroad for a week or two of holiday; it's quite another to do so for months or years at a time.

The Buy-to-let Option

Some people fancy the idea of becoming property barons by gradually buying up flats or houses, renting them out and using the income to pay off mortgages and build equity. Within a few years – so the theory goes – one will own a collection of properties unencumbered by debt and perhaps be able to live off the income they generate.

It's a good theory, and it has been known to work. But once again, careful planning is essential. The rental market today is much weaker than it was a few years ago. Rents haven't been rising as steadily as they did in the 1990s; in fact, they fell by 20% between 2002 and 2003. So for many landlords, buy-to-let has turned into buy-to-fret.

The first key is to choose a property in the right neighbourhood, one where there is a limited supply of new homes and a demand for rental housing. Your best bet is probably not a family house with garden (since most people who are attracted to such properties are eager to buy rather than rent) but an easy-to-maintain city-centre apartment (which will appeal to young people or to those who plan to stay for just a year or two before moving on).

Once you've researched the best areas and found yourself a perfect rental property, your next step is to find a buy-to-let mortgage. Most lenders now offer almost their full range of products as buy-to-let, but the interest rates might be higher, and they will probably offer to lend no more than 75–85% of the property's value. Buy-to-let is considered higher risk for the lender than an ordinary mortgage, as tenants won't care for a place in the same way that an owner would.

Next, consider whether the type of tenant you seek will want furnished or unfurnished accommodation. If you decide to furnish, buy plain, reasonable-quality furnishings and expect to replace them every few years.

Set your rental charges so as to cover possible increases in interest rates that could push up your monthly mortgage payments. As a rule of thumb, try to achieve rental income that totals around 140% of your mortgage payments while allowing for two months without tenants each year. So if your mortgage payment is £500 a month (£6,000 a year), you'll want an annual rental income of £8,400 (since £6,000 × 140% = £8,400). Now, to earn that in ten months (allowing for two months' vacancy), you'll have to charge rent of £840 a month.

Is this a fair rent for the property? The only way to be sure is to research the area. Visit other properties that are priced about the same and compare them to the property you are considering. If the size and quality of the space you are offering is similar, then you have *priced to market*. If not, you may have trouble recouping your costs.

The administrative and managerial tasks associated with renting property can be burdensome. You'll have to attract and screen potential tenants, collect the rent and pursue non-payers. You'll have to deal with emergencies ranging from a broken refrigerator to a leaky ceiling. You'll need proper legal leases, and you'll have to fill out your tax return and pay tax on the rental income earned (after any deductible expenses).

Is the potential income from property rental enough to make

this worthwhile? That's up to you. Some landlords choose to employ letting agents to handle much of the administrative work of property rental. The agent will generally charge a minimum of 10% of all rent collected for basic service and at least 15% for full management – a cost that must be factored in when determining the income needed to make your property business profitable.

Buy-to-let property has one great advantage: namely, the historic tendency of property values to increase over time. Thus, if you've managed the business wisely, while your tenants are covering your costs and providing a little profit, the value of the property should also be rising. The big pay-off will come years down the road, when you sell the property at a handsome profit.

But remember that property investment is not risk-free. What goes up can also come down. Even in a rising market, it may take years before the value of your property increases enough to cover all the costs of buying and selling (including stamp duty when you buy and capital gains tax when you sell). And don't underestimate the deterioration most rental properties suffer. To lessen these risks of landlordship, you should keep a contingency fund of six months' rent in a savings account to cover emergencies like a boiler breakdown or a period of months without tenants.

I don't mean to discourage you from thinking about buy-to-let as a possible investment, but I *do* want you to realise that it's not a path to risk-free, no-work income. Being a landlord is like most other jobs – it's potentially rewarding, but it demands intelligent planning and hard work.

Flipping Out – Buying to Develop

One of the latest trends to hit reality TV is the craze for *flipping* properties – buying them, fixing them up or developing them and reselling them for a profit. After a series of such flips, a relatively modest initial investment can become huge . . . provided that everything works according to plan. In the programme *The Million Pound Property Experiment*, Colin McAllister and Justin Ryan managed to turn a £100,000 investment into more than a million in just seven property transactions – but only with the help of a great professional team of top architects, designers, developers, builders and estate agents, plus a flexible bankroll from the BBC. And even then, everything that possibly could go wrong *did* go wrong.

My friend Michelle and her sister have immersed themselves in property development, so much of the advice here comes from them, for which I give grateful thanks. Here are their insights into how the professionals actually go about buying, upgrading and reselling propeties for profit:

- Successful property development requires detailed knowledge of the area in which you're buying and a clear profile of the prospective buyer. Are you planning to sell the property to a City whiz-kid who wants low maintenance and all mod cons as well as impressive design features? To a family of four who want plenty of play space and an easy-to-keep garden? Or to a girl-about-town who needs masses of storage space for her designer wardrobe? Start by identifying your target buyers and develop and decorate with them in mind.
- As always, location is key. Your best bet is a run-down property in a top-notch area – one you can buy cheap, do up and sell dear. Second best is a property on the edge of a top-notch area that's ready to expand. Trouble is, only the very experienced (and lucky) can predict tomorrow's up-and-coming neighbourhoods. So buying low and selling high is easier said than done.
- Space expansion can make a property's value grow. If you can add an extension, knock through an underused utility room to make a garage or turn a patio space into a new sun-lit sitting room, you may have a winner.
- Oversee any building work yourself and manage the budget every single day. Get several quotes for each job, and always allow a contingency fund of at least 25%. Cost overruns are inevitable.
- Time overruns are also inevitable. Unfortunately, while the renovation drags on, you will be making mortgage payments

every month, taking profit off the bottom line. If you run into a slow-selling period like the Christmas holidays, you could lose several months before the market picks up again.

All of this means that you will have to achieve a hefty profit to cover all your expenses, including transaction costs such as stamp duty and capital gains tax. You should also consider the time you are investing as a cost. (Believe me, you will be spending much more time on the building site than you expect.) If you clear £20,000 profit after six months' full-time work, will you be happy with that?

Buy-to-develop is nerve-racking and demanding, but property can produce very good returns if you do your sums carefully and are prepared to get your hands dirty doing some of the work yourself. I know some people who manage mini-empires of up to ten properties. They clear enough to pay their kids' school fees on the annual profits, while the long-term increase in capital value will eventually boost their retirement funds. But not one of them would ever say it's been easy money.

7 | MANAGING YOUR HOME EQUITY

For millions of British families, the value of their homes is the greatest mass of wealth they'll ever achieve. This makes it very tempting to take some of that equity and turn it into cash that can be spent on education, travel, furniture and other accoutrements of the good life. But is this wise? When is it prudent to dip into your home equity, and when should it be avoided? In this chapter, I'll offer some guidelines that will help you develop your own answers to these important questions as well as to other issues related to managing the finances of homeownership.

Taking Equity Out of Your Home

In 2003, £53 billion was borrowed in the UK against property equity. That's about £2,000 per household – a fair sum of money by any standard. Is this trend a healthy one? Should *your* family jump on the bandwagon? It depends on your specific circumstances. But let's start our analysis by clearing away some common misunderstandings.

Some people think of the equity in their home as *their* money and feel frustrated that they can't immediately lay their hands on it. 'What's the point in owning a home that's worth £200,000 if I can't touch a penny of it?' they wonder. And they complain, 'I'm house-rich but cash-poor.'

Financial institutions have rushed in with a solution to this 'problem': the *second mortgage* or *home-equity loan*. It's presented to homeowners as a way of 'unlocking the hidden value' in their property – almost like some sort of wonderful conjuring trick. But when you take advantage of the home-equity deals being offered by finance companies, you are *borrowing* the money. The interest rate on the loan may be relatively favourable (compared to overdrafts or credit cards), but it's a loan all the same, and it will have to be repaid – with interest. Either your monthly mortgage payments will increase or you will have additional payments to make. Equity is *not* your money until you sell the property, at which point you will probably need it to fund your next home purchase.

Of course, I'm not opposed to all borrowing. Most people need a mortgage loan to buy their home in the first place, and within reason it's a sensible way to borrow. However, I strongly suggest that you do *not* commit more than 30% of your monthly take-home pay to mortgage payments – and that includes any second mortgages or loans secured against your home. If increasing your mortgage would take your repayments over that level, then don't do it!

Sometimes borrowing against your home is presented as a part of a programme for debt reduction. When filming my TV show *Your Money or Your Life*, I often came across people deep in debt who'd consolidated all their borrowing into a single low-interest loan secured against their property. In fact, many debt advisers recommend this as a way out of financial trouble. The idea is to eliminate eight or ten debts (to credit-card companies, department stores, finance companies and the like) and replace them with a single home-equity loan, often at a lower interest rate. The single monthly payment is generally less than the total of the many consolidated bills (although it must be paid over a longer period of time). It's not a bad idea as far as it goes. But the advisers who promote this plan aren't making allowances for human psychology. People who are deep in debt have trouble controlling their spending. As soon as they consolidate their borrowing into a single loan, they usually start running up new balances on their credit cards and store cards. Soon they are buried under a pile of bills very much like the ones they carried before – only now they have a big home-equity debt to repay as well!

I recommend the debt-consolidation route only to people who have got into debt due to exceptional circumstances –

being made redundant, for example. I tell them to work out a frugal monthly budget and really stick to it. And I urge them not to use any other form of credit until the home-equity loan is paid off. If necessary, take a pair of scissors to the credit cards.

So if you are *very* disciplined, you might consider extending your mortgage to consolidate debts or perhaps to manage an extraordinary expense – a new roof or a medical emergency, for instance. But I would never borrow against my home to pay for a holiday, a car or any other non-essential item. In the long run, the debt will be too costly and too risky.

Equity-release Schemes

Perhaps you've heard about *equity-release schemes*. They generally take two different forms. Here's how they work:

- An *interest roll-up loan* allows you to borrow a lump sum against the equity in your home. However, you make no repayments during your lifetime. Instead, the interest is added to the loan ('rolled up'), and the total borrowed is taken out of your home's value when the home is sold after your death.
- A *home-reversion scheme* allows you to sell all or part of your home in return for a lump sum and/or monthly income. You will usually receive only 40–60% of your home's full value, although you will be allowed to continue living there.

Equity-release schemes were originally devised as a way of allowing elderly people to exchange some of their home equity in return for a lump sum or a monthly income. Unfortunately, these schemes don't generally provide very good value for money and have several serious drawbacks:

- They reduce your flexibility if, say, you want to move to a different house in the future.
- There are early repayment penalties if you decide you want to pay off an interest roll-up loan. The interest rates are usually high, and there are arrangement, legal and survey fees to cover.
- If you sell your home under a home-reversion scheme, you're still responsible for maintaining the property, and the lender will check that you are doing so.
- If you want income from the lump sum released, you often have to buy an annuity from the lender, which may not be the best-value annuity on the market. If you die soon thereafter, your descendants will receive nothing.
- Any lump sum or income you receive could reduce your entitlement to state benefits.

The Financial Services Authority categorises equity-release schemes as 'high risk'. For all these reasons, I would consider an equity-release scheme only as a last resort. If you badly need a lump sum, it would be far better to *sell down* the property ladder: sell your present home and then buy somewhere smaller and less costly. The difference in price is yours, with no strings attached.

When You Can't Keep Up With the Repayments

If you're finding it hard to meet your mortgage payments every month, the first thing to do is figure out why. The reason may be obvious: a lost job, a major illness or a serious accident. If the reason isn't obvious, examine your monthly spending patterns closely. Use recent bank statements and credit-card bills to figure out where the money is going and to identify categories where you could cut back. Are there luxuries you can give up? Perhaps spending £10 less here and £20 less there will add up over the course of a month into the savings needed to meet your mortgage obligations.

Also look at the income side of the ledger. Can you take steps to increase your cash flow? Consider taking on a second job, working overtime or starting a small business on the side using any talent you have that is saleable.

If you find yourself getting into mortgage arrears, don't let things slide. This is one situation where the natural human instinct to *avoid trouble* can do you harm. Rather than withdrawing into denial, face the problem head on. Start by getting in touch with your mortgage lender and explaining the situation. Describe the problem that has caused you to fall behind, explain your willingness to work out a solution and ask for help. Your lender will almost certainly try to be accommodating. The type of arrangements lenders can offer to an over-extended borrower include the following:

- On a repayment mortgage, they may offer to let you pay interest only until your finances are repaired.
- They may extend the period of the loan or lower the interest rate to reduce monthly payments in the short term.
- With a flexible mortgage, you can take a payment holiday, but you'll have to pay extra to catch up later.

Mortgage lenders are much more likely to negotiate a fair deal if they can see you are trying hard to help yourself. For example, if you take on some cab-driving work in the evenings while you are job-hunting or sub-let a room in your house, you will prove to them that you are serious about paying off your debts.

If your arrears keep mounting and repossession of your home by the lender is looming, your best bet is to sell the property yourself, pay off the loan and either buy or rent something cheaper.

If the lender takes legal action to reposess you, get legal representation (or contact your local Citizens Advice Bureau if you cannot afford it), attend the court hearing and make sure the judge is aware of any extenuating evidence. For example, if you've been unemployed but have recently managed to find work, if you have a young family to support, if you care for an elderly or disabled relative, or if you've had an accident or serious illness, the judge may show some leniency.

If the court agrees to the repossession order, you will have just 14 days to move out. The lender will then put your house on the market, possibly at auction, to pay off what you owe, including the unpaid mortgage debt and the lender's legal costs. Unfortunately, the empty property is unlikely to achieve the full price it could have attained if you had sold it yourself as outlined in Chapter 5. If the property is sold for less than what you owe, the lender can pursue you for repayment of the shortfall for up to 12 years after the sale. You will also have some seriously black marks on your credit rating.

Don't think you will be protected if you paid for a higher lending charge (HLC). After repossession, the MIG insurer will make up any shortfall to the lender, but they will then have the right to pursue you for the money. Get legal advice if you find yourself faced with mortgage-shortfall debt after a repossession.

Bankruptcy, of course, is the ultimate loss of financial control and independence. What does it mean to you as a homeowner?

If you owe creditors a substantial amount of money, they can ask the court to put a *charging order* on your home. This means that they will be reimbursed from the proceeds when you eventually sell the property. In effect, this changes an unsecured loan into a secured one. If you don't keep up with any negotiated repayment plan, the creditor could then apply to the court to force you to sell the property. (You might also get a charging order placed on your property if you are in conflict with an ex-partner or have an unresolved inheritance dispute.)

After reading the last few pages, you're probably feeling quite nervous. Obviously, the consequences if you don't keep up with mortgage repayments can be very severe. Follow my advice by building a savings cushion and handling debt and spending prudently, and you will never find yourself in this situation.

When Equity Turns Negative

If there's a slump in property prices – which does happen from time to time – you may find yourself in possession of a house that's worth less than what you owe on your mortgage. This situation is called *negative equity*. It means that, if you sell the property, you won't collect enough to pay off your mortgage debt. What should you do if this happens?

If you weren't planning to move, good! The best thing to do when your home equity is negative is simply to stay put. Over the long term, property values tend to rise. So if you can wait, the chances are very good that, eventually, your home's value will rise to the point where you have positive equity and can safely think about selling.

Unfortunately, it can take quite a while for prices to recover. A friend of mine who got caught in the property collapse of the early 1990s had to wait five years before he could sell his flat for the amount he had paid for it.

What if you have no choice but to sell? (For example, suppose your employer sends you to live and work in a distant city, which forces you to pull up stakes and buy a new home elsewhere.) Your won't be able to redeem your current mortgage until you find a lump sum to make up the shortfall. Talk to several lenders to explore possible solutions. For instance, you may be able to get a 100% mortgage on a second property and take out a loan to cover the negative equity on the first. But it's a risky approach that will seriously stretch your finances, so I wouldn't recommend this route if you have any other option.

The best advice is avoid being caught in the negative-equity trap in the first place. Whenever you buy a property, put down a deposit of at least 20% of its value. This greatly reduces the likelihood that any drop in property values will push you into negative territory.

Endowment Shortfall

If you have an endowment mortgage (as described in Chapter 2), you may be one of the tens of thousands who have received an ominous letter telling you that your investments are unlikely to pay off the capital sum at the end of the term. If you threw this letter into a pile of other mail and promptly forgot about it, dig it out now and take action – fast! You only have three years from your first letter warning about a shortfall (often called a 'red' warning letter) to make a complaint.

First of all, try to locate the original documents you signed when you took out the mortgage. Check whether there is any small print anywhere warning you that the value of endowments is linked to stock-market performance and that there is a risk that they may not increase sufficiently to raise the sum you need. If this risk was expressed in writing at the time you bought the policy, you have no one to blame but yourself. However, if it wasn't – and many policies sold in the late 1980s and early 1990s failed to point this out – then you must complain now. You have three years from the date of the first letter warning you that your endowment isn't on target, so act quickly.

Write first to the company that sold you the endowment mortgage. Say that you wish to complain because the risks were not made clear at the time of your mortgage purchase. They will almost certainly have a standard complaints procedure, which you'll want to follow precisely. Keep copies of every document and respond promptly to every request for information.

If the mortgage company rejects your complaint, you can take matters to the Financial Ombudsman Service, which offers a free service aimed at resolving disputes about complaints.

If your complaint is upheld, you will be offered compensation, amounting, perhaps, to a few thousand pounds, which is certainly better than nothing.

Next, you must decide how you are going to pay off your mortgage balance. You have a few options:

- You can switch from an interest-only mortgage to a repayment mortgage. Use an online mortgage calculator or speak to an advisor at your mortgage company to figure out how much more your monthly payments would be. However, in many cases it will be better, keep paying into your endowment than cash it in (although there are a few policies where returns are so low this may not be the case). If you cash endowments in early, all the charges will have been deducted but the interest won't have had sufficient time to build up.
- If you can't afford the full cost of a repayment mortgage, consider switching *part* of your mortgage to repayment. For example, suppose you have a £100,000 mortgage and your endowment is currently projected to pay £60,000. You could switch £40,000 of your mortgage to repayment and keep £60,000 as interest only. However, you'll want to keep an eye on the value of your endowments and be prepared to switch more over to repayment if necessary.
- You can set up some other kind of investment plan to make up the shortfall. For example, you could use your ISA entitlement to buy tax-free investments to top up your mortgage at the end of the term. (You can put up to £5,000 a year in a stocks and shares maxi ISA.) However, be aware

that maxi ISAs are stock-market investments, just like endowments, and there is no guarantee that your money will grow fast enough to pay off your mortgage capital at the end of the term.

Whatever you do, you must do *something*. You don't want to pass retirement age and still have mortgage payments to meet.

Is Your Home Your Pension?

I meet many people in Britain who tell me that 'their home is their pension'. This can be a very dangerous way of thinking, and I want to explain why.

As I've repeatedly noted, property does tend to increase in value over time, so long as it's well maintained and located in an area where other people want to live. But there can be slumps, and if you need to sell your home in the middle of one, you'll lose money.

Many members of the generation now reaching retirement age enjoyed enormous profits from their ownership of property. Some of them paid amounts like £2,000 or £4,000 in the 1950s or 1960s for houses now valued at £250,000 or more. That kind of gigantic increase won't happen if you bought in the 1980s, 1990s or 2000s. It was an aberration, caused in large part by the dramatic post-war recovery into you've-never-had-it-so-good prosperity. In the decades to come, homeowners can expect property values to increase by single figures, rather than the double digits we saw a generation ago.

This is one reason why, for most Britons, it's unrealistic to imagine that your home will be your pension. Another is that, for as long as you live, you'll need a home of some sort. Therefore, when you eventually sell your house, you'll need enough cash to buy or rent somewhere else to live. And unless you trade down *very* significantly, you will never be able to release enough cash to fund your old age.

For example, suppose you sell one property, buy a smaller one and manage to free up £100,000 worth of equity. At current annuity rates, this would buy you around £6,000 a year of annual income. Could you live on that? Not very well, I imagine.

So don't think of your primary residence as an investment. Instead, consider it a home. Make sure your mortgage is on track to pay off the capital sum you owe. Then you'll enjoy cheap accommodation for life. And after you die, you can pass the home on to your loved ones to help them to consolidate their financial security.

As for your pension, develop a separate savings and investment plan for that. Put money into a bank account, bonds, shares, unit trusts and other proven financial instruments. (My book *Save and Invest with Alvin Hall* offers much more detail.) Managed wisely, such a pension plan can offer you the secure old age that a home is unlikely ever to provide.

Where There's a Will

Someday – many, many years from today, I trust – you will grow old and die. When that happens, you owe it to your loved ones to have a plan in place concerning the inheritance of your money and other assets, including any property you own.

Inheritance planning is an important and complex topic in its own right, but over the next couple of pages, I'll offer a brief introduction to how it relates to property ownership.

In the UK, the inheritance tax threshold is currently set at £285,000, meaning that only estates with a greater value are subject to tax on the death of the owner. Given the way property values have increased in recent decades, many family homes now push the estate over the tax threshold. Note that there is no tax due on property that passes between husband and wife, but if you want the family home to go to your children, you could be bequeathing them a massive tax bill along with the intended nest egg.

If you are in this situation, it's worth consulting a lawyer who specialises in estate planning to develop a tax-minimisation strategy, particularly if you want your heirs to avoid having to sell the home to pay taxes. You can't simply put the house in the name of your child and hope thereby to escape inheritance tax, since the law has been written to recognise this as a tax-avoidance strategy and has closed the loophole. In recent years, a numbe rof similar loopholes have been closed, so it is worth remembering that what is leagl today may not be tomorrow. But one route to consider is passing the house to your children under the control of a trust while you are still alive. You can remain in the house, paying rent to the trust for the privilege. Remember, your children will own your house, so you must feel confident that they will always have your best interests at heart. And for the scheme to comply with tax laws, you have to pay the full market rent, not a nominal amount. There are also special life-insurance policies designed to help defray the expense of inheritance tax, permitting the rest of your estate to be transmitted free and clear. Again, all of these estate-planning strategies require advice from an expert.

In any case, it's crucial that you work with a lawyer to make a will. Otherwise, you can't guarantee that your property will go to the person you choose. If you want to avoid your family battling in court for years after your passing, pay a couple of hundred pounds now to make your wishes crystal clear and legally binding.

Leave a copy of your will in a place where your heirs will find it. It would also be helpful to leave them a house logbook of the type I discussed on page 71. They won't be able to phone you in heaven to find out who the building insurers are or when the central heating was last serviced. Set aside a drawer in a filing cabinet or in your desk for property-related paperwork, including planning permissions, legal documents, mortgage payments and other information. Even as your heirs mourn your loss, they will be thanking you for your foresight.

Index

accidents 107, 109
Alvin Hall's Guide to Successful Investing (TV series) 4
arrangement fee 25
Association of Private Client Investment Managers and Stockbrokers (APCIMS) 31
Association of Solicitors and Investment Managers (ASIM) 31
auctions 46–7

bad-credit risk 30–32
bank accounts 116
Bank of England 24
bank loans 8
bankruptcies 14, 109–110
base rate 24
bonds 9, 116
bridging loans 83–4
buy-to-let option 95–9
buyers' market 12

capped rate 25
chain-breaking loans 83, 84
cohabitation agreements 12, 54–5
community charge 50
completion 57, 58
construction quality 22
contents insurance 56
conveyancing 48–9
cost-cutting programme 17–18
county court judgements 9
credit cards 8, 14, 17, 104, 107
credit rating 8–9, 109

debt
 clearing 8
 consolidation 104–5
 consumer 14
 unmanageable 3
disability 8, 12
discount rate 25

INDEX 119

early repayment penalties 25–6
education 10, 20, 21, 22, 86
emergency savings fund 7, 9, 11
Equifax credit agency 8
equity *see* home equity management
estate agents 42, 43, 58, 77–80, 85, 86, 87
Ethical Investment Research Service (EIRIS) 31
exchange of contracts 56, 57
expenses, regular 11–12
Experian credit agency 8

family life 10–11
Financial Services Authority (FSA) 32, 89, 106, 113
fixed rate 24–5
freehold property 48, 50
friend, buying with a 55
FTSE All-share Index 2
full building survey 52–3

gazumping 44–6, 87
ground rent 50

Hall, Alvin
 Get Out of Debt with Alvin Hall 8
 Save and Invest with Alvin Hall 116
home equity management 102–118
 endowment shortfall 112–14

equity-release schemes 105–7
inability to keep up with repayments 107–110
inheritance planning 114–16
negative equity 65, 110–112
taking equity out of your home 102–5
your home as your pension 114–16
home improvements 59–72
 adding value by redecorating 62–5
 keeping up appearances 71–2
 paying for home improvements 65–8
 the renovation adventure 67–8
 take it slow 60–62
 working with building professionals 68–70
home information packs 22, 45–6, 80–81
home-equity loan 103
homebuyer's survey 53
house logbook 71–2, 117–18
housing associations 108

illness 8, 12, 106, 107
income protection 7–8
income security 7–8
inheritance planning 114–16
Institute of Financial Planning (IFP) 31–2
interest rates 15–16
ISAs 39, 114

joint freeholders 51

Land Registry 48, 49
Law Society 48
leasehold property 48, 50–51
life-insurance companies 27
life-insurance policies 117
listed buildings 68
loan repayments, defaulting on 9
Local Authority Building Control 67–8
London Stock Exchange 2

McAllister, Colin and Ryan, Justin: *The Million Pound Property Experiment* 99
maternity leave 10
mortgage brokers 30–32
mortgage indemnity guarantee (MIG) 11, 109
mortgage principal 26, 28
mortgage protection insurance 37
mortgage valuation 51–2, 53
mortgage-shopping tips 37–9
mortgages
  100 36–7
  cashback 33
  deposit 11
  endowment 27, 28, 112–14
  flexible 33–4
  impaired credit (adverse-credit) 35–6
  interest rates 15–16, 24–6, 40
  interest-only 26–8

  missed payments 17
  mortgage term options 29
  online mortgage calculators 14, 15, 16
  pension 28
  repayment 26, 27, 28, 113–14
  second 103
  self-certification 34–5
  size of 10–11, 13–16
  and unemployment 8
moving up the ladder 73–87
  the art of the close 86–7
  be your own agent 81–2
  estate agents 77–80
  having trouble selling 84–6
  home information pack 80–81
  prepping your place to sell 74–6
  when a deal breaks down 82–4

National Association of Estate Agents 79
National Federation of Builders 69
negative equity 65, 110–112
note of interest 46

offer on a home 42–4
Ombudsman for Estate Agents Scheme 79
overdrafts 8
overseas properties 93–5

partner, buying with a 54–5
pension plan 9–10, 28, 39, 116

poor credit risks 9
pressure to buy 5–6
property insurance 56
property investments 2, 88–101
   buy-to-let option 95–9
   buying to develop 99–101
   drawbacks 89–90
   overseas 93–5
   second homes 90–92
property shopping 19–22
property values 2, 7, 12, 110–112

ready to buy? 6–13
redundancy 105
relationships 11, 54, 55
remortgages 27, 28, 39–41
renting 2, 3–5, 7, 13, 18–19, 86
   buy-to-let option 95–9
repossessions 3, 108, 109
Royal Institute of Chartered
   Surveyors 53, 79
Ryan, Justin *see* McAllister, Colin

savings account 39
second homes 90–92
security of home ownership 2, 3
self-employed 7–8, 30, 34, 35

sellers' market 12
service charge 50
shares 9, 39, 116
sole selling-rights 78–9
solicitors 46, 48–50, 58
stamp duty 57–8
   threshold 15
stock market 27–8
stocks 39
store cards 8, 104
structural survey 52–3
student loans 8
surveys 51–3, 86, 87

term of the mortgage 26
tracker rate 24

unemployment 8, 12, 107, 109
unit trusts 39, 116

variable interest rate 24, 25

websites 46
wills 117

Your Money or Your Life (TV show)
   104